Ending Violent Conflict

MICHAEL RENNER

Daniel Schwartz, *Research Intern*

Jane A. Peterson, *Editor*

WORLDWATCH PAPER 146

April 1999

THE WORLDWATCH INSTITUTE is an independent, nonprofit environmental research organization in Washington, DC. Its mission is to foster a sustainable society in which human needs are met in ways that do not threaten the health of the natural environment or future generations. To this end, the Institute conducts interdisciplinary research on emerging global issues, the results of which are published and disseminated to decision-makers and the media.

FINANCIAL SUPPORT for the Institute is provided by the Geraldine R. Dodge Foundation, the Ford Foundation, the William and Flora Hewlett Foundation, W. Alton Jones Foundation, Charles Stewart Mott Foundation, the Curtis and Edith Munson Foundation, David and Lucile Packard Foundation, Rasmussen Foundation, Rockefeller Financial Services, Summit Foundation, Turner Foundation, U.N. Population Fund, Wallace Genetic Foundation, Wallace Global Fund, Weeden Foundation, and the Winslow Foundation.

THE WORLDWATCH PAPERS provide in-depth, quantitative and qualitative analysis of the major issues affecting prospects for a sustainable society. The Papers are written by members of the Worldwatch Institute research staff and reviewed by experts in the field. Published in five languages, they have been used as concise and authoritative references by governments, nongovernmental organizations, and educational institutions worldwide. For a partial list of available Papers, see back pages.

REPRINT AND COPYRIGHT INFORMATION for one-time academic use of this material is available by contacting Customer Service, Copyright Clearance Center, at (978) 750-8400 (phone), or (978) 750-4744 (fax), or writing to CCC, 222 Rosewood Drive, Danvers, MA 01923. Nonacademic users should call the Worldwatch Institute's Communication Department at (202) 452-1992, x517, or fax a request to (202) 296-7365.

Table of Contents

ACKNOWLEDGMENTS: I am grateful to all of my fellow Worldwatch researchers for comments on an early draft of this paper and numerous suggestions for improvements. I am particularly indebted to Chris Flavin for providing valuable feedback throughout the research, writing, and editing stages. Daniel Schwartz provided research support, tracking down books, reports, and data in astonishingly short time. Special thanks are due to Jane Peterson for her gentle and consistent style that turns editing and proofreading from a dreaded task into an enjoyable process; to Liz Doherty, who turned messy manuscript pages into galleys and page proofs in amazingly little time, even as she juggled three other projects; to Payal Sampat and Lisa Mastny for reviewing galleys; to Amy Warehime for keeping us all to the agreed production schedule; and to Dick Bell, Mary Caron, and Alison Trice for their tireless outreach and communications work. Most of all, my appreciation goes to my wife, Annette, and my children, Paul and Judith, for making sure that I kept things in perspective even when deadlines seemed tight and impossible to meet.

MICHAEL RENNER joined the Worldwatch staff in 1987 and is currently a Senior Researcher. He is the author of seven previous Worldwatch Papers, including *Small Arms, Big Impact: The Next Challenge of Disarmament* (October 1997), and *Fighting for Survival: Environmental Decline, Social Conflict, and the New Age of Insecurity*, published by W.W. Norton in 1996. Renner has been a co-author of Worldwatch's annual *State of the World* reports since 1989 and has served as associate project director for the Institute's other annual, *Vital Signs*, since 1997. He holds degrees in international relations and political science from the Universities of Amsterdam, Netherlands, and Konstanz, Germany.

A Centennial Perspective

As we come to the conclusion of the most war-ravaged century in human history, there are eerie parallels with the world of 100 years ago. At the end of the last century, the predominant mood in Europe was one of enormous optimism, supported by a sense of the inevitability of human progress driven by rapid technological and economic advances. The fact that war among the major powers had been absent for about three decades also seemed reason for confidence. And liberal economists further shored up this sanguine outlook, claiming that intensified international trade and finance would preclude war.

But other contemporaries grew apprehensive as the military expenditures of the six leading European powers tripled and the size of their armies doubled between 1880 and 1914. Swedish industrialist Alfred Nobel, inventor of dynamite, was deeply pessimistic, but he nevertheless banked on an idea that foreshadowed the nuclear deterrence school of thought—that the destructive power of new armaments was so immense as to render future warfare unthinkable.[1]

Nobel was a close friend of Bertha von Suttner, a leading pacifist of the time who encouraged him to devote his wealth to the cause of peace and who herself became a Nobel Peace Prize recipient in 1905. Von Suttner argued passionately for the establishment of an organization like the United Nations, for the creation of what we now call peacekeeping forces, and for a "European Confederation of States." She marshaled a mixture of realism—the ability to comprehend the consequences of the trends of her time—

and vision—the ability to see clearly what must be done—
that embodied hope for a better future.[2]

Von Suttner and other pacifists persuaded Czar
Nicholas II of Russia, who was worried about the "crushing
burden" of the "armed peace of our days," to convene the
First Hague International Peace Conference in the
Netherlands in 1899. This seminal event brought together
government representatives from 26 nations—a large pro-
portion of the sovereign states that existed then. It was the
first conference ever called to seek ways to reduce the likelihood of war, rather than to distribute its spoils.[3]

But although the 1899 conference and a follow-up
gathering in 1907 succeeded in codifying some rules for con-
ducting war, they failed to make significant headway toward
preventing conflict. An arbitration court was set up, but its use
remained entirely voluntary. A Russian proposal for a five-
year moratorium on arms purchases was rejected, and an
opportunity to ban aerial warfare—which was to make its
debut in the Italian-Turkish war of 1911—was missed.[4]

The steady buildup of arms in Europe intensified after
the turn of the century. But even after fighting broke out in
August 1914, virtually everyone assumed that this war would
be short, just as the Franco-Prussian War nearly half a century earlier had been. Still hopeful, they believed that the soldiers would be home by Christmas. Few imagined that they
were on the verge of the most devastating war in history—or
that it would be followed by an even larger global conflict
less than three decades later.[5]

Today, the knowledge of utter devastation wreaked by
two lengthy world wars, and the threat of total annihilation
in a nuclear holocaust have shattered many illusions about
the "glory" of war that were strongly held a century ago. The
promise of a more peaceful future is once again clouded by
uncertainties ahead, just as it was at the time of the Hague
Peace Conference. Will the new century be as violent as the
old, the most destructive age ever? Or will humanity finally
summon the ability to tame the beast of war?

Having witnessed the astronomical scale of human

conflict, we find ourselves facing a most unusual situation: the absence of any big-power confrontation. The leading nations of Europe, where so many wars of the past originated, today enjoy cordial relations. The world as a whole is moving rapidly toward ever-increasing economic integration, giving rise to the hope—much like that of a century ago—that economic interest will trump belligerence. And we have made halting progress toward laws governing war (the so-called humanitarian laws), toward arms control, peacekeeping, and institutions to help govern international relations.

Yet dangers lurk today as yesterday. The Gulf War of 1991 was an early reminder that the end of the Cold War did not signal permanent peace. And while there have been relatively few interstate wars since then, deadly internal conflicts are common, as seen most recently in the Balkans. These conflicts are primarily fought with small-caliber arms and other relatively unsophisticated weapons. But because there is no distinct battlefield, fighters range over large areas, often targeting civilian populations for killings, terror, and expulsions. Such wars visit enormous devastation upon affected territories.

Many of today's wars are the product of accumulating social, economic, demographic, and environmental pressures. In this, too, there is a similarity to the situation a century ago: in 1914, the inescapable stresses created by population growth and the strains of rapid urbanization and industrialization were channeled into an unquestioning patriotism, which underpinned the ardor that swept Europe into war. Today, such stress factors more often lead to internal conflicts than to wars of state against state. But far from being limited in their impact, internal wars may trigger the collapse of entire societies, destabilize neighboring countries through massive outflows of refugees, and prompt foreign intervention. Somalia, Rwanda, Bosnia, and Kosovo may only be harbingers of conflicts to come.[6]

At the threshold of the twenty-first century, we thus face a choice: Will we be overwhelmed by an endless string of internal wars capable of devastating entire countries and perhaps even re-igniting interstate confrontations, or will we build the foundations for a lasting peace? Will we seize the opportunity offered by the absence of big-power rivalries and retain control of our destinies? Or will we let unanticipated events such as the Sarajevo assassination in 1914 determine the future of peace and war, allowing the logic of military imperatives to dictate political considerations?[7]

Governments still devote far less energy and enthusiasm to the task of conflict prevention and peace-building than to war preparation and war-making. Existing international institutions—foremost among them the United Nations—are too weak to prevent war. Humanity is ill-equipped, then, at this millennial moment, to handle either a resurgence of interstate war, should it happen, or an unending series of internal wars.

The challenge is twofold. One is to fortify the nascent infrastructure of peace—promoting disarmament, building conflict prevention networks, advancing human rights law, and strengthening peacekeeping capacities. Of particular urgency is the need to reduce the abundance of arms of virtually all calibers, a lingering legacy of the twentieth century. As long as weapons are readily available, there will always be a temptation to rely on them to settle disputes rather than to engage in the arduous task of negotiating and arbitrating conflicting needs and interests.

The second challenge is to understand and address the underlying causes of today's conflicts, including poverty, social inequality, ethnic tensions, population growth, and environmental degradation. These pressures appear to be accelerating in many societies even as governance structures falter. Left unaddressed, it is likely that they will heighten polarization and instability, possibly leading to widespread violent conflict.

One hundred years after the first Hague conference, in May 1999, the Hague Appeal for Peace is bringing together hundreds of peace, human rights, environmental, and other grassroots and advocacy groups as well as thousands of citizen activists to develop a twenty-first-century agenda for peace and justice. Its mission is to address the unfinished business of its predecessor, to seek the prevention and resolution of violent conflict, far-reaching disarmament, the further development of international humanitarian and human rights law, and the promotion of a worldwide culture of peace. It also signals a new era: this time around, it is nongovernmental groups (NGOs), not governments, that are meeting to set an agenda for peace in the new century.[8]

The 1999 Hague gathering provides evidence that growing numbers of people reject the notion that went almost unchallenged in Bertha von Suttner's day—that "war," as German general von Moltke said, "is an element in God's order." By now it is clear that war is neither holy nor inevitable. Under the right circumstances—with policies that defuse rather than aggravate conflicts—war can be abolished.[9]

The Toll of Modern Wars

When Europe plunged into the abyss in August 1914, the British Secretary of State for Foreign Affairs, Sir Edward Grey, sensed that life as he knew it was about to be swept away. "The lamps are going out all over Europe," he observed; "we shall not see them lit again in our lifetime." Indeed, the war would wreak unprecedented destruction and spark revolutions and unrest across the continent.[10]

Although militarism was deeply ingrained in the cultures of many societies 100 years ago, the preambles of nineteenth century humanitarian law nevertheless frequently invoked the need for civilized society to restrain warfare. For instance, the 1868 St. Petersburg "Declaration Renouncing the Use, in Time of War, of Certain Explosive Projectiles" recognized that there was a point "at which the necessities of war ought to yield to the requirements of humanity."[11]

During the twentieth century, however, combatants have ignored these admonitions, wreaking killings, expulsions, and wholesale destruction with such ruthlessness and on such a vast scale that new words had to be invented to capture them. The term *genocide* was coined in 1944 to describe the deliberate and systematic destruction of a racial, political, or cultural group. And in 1957, *overkill* was first used to mean using far greater destructive force than required to obliterate a target. Until the sixteenth century, fewer than 1 million persons were killed in battle or due to war-related causes, such as hunger and disease, during any 100-year stretch. From then on, the pace accelerated. Three times as many people fell victim to war in our century as in all the wars from the first century AD to 1899. (See Table 1.)[12]

So extensive was the killing during World War I that individual battles inflicted casualties as large as those suffered in entire wars of earlier eras. (See Table 2.) By 1918, the French had lost almost 20 percent of their men of military age, the Germans 13 percent. All in all, an estimated 26 million people died during the "Great War"; at least another 20 million or so were maimed, disabled, or permanently shellshocked. Due mainly to malnutrition and lack of medical care, civilians accounted for half of all war deaths.[13]

One reason World War I was so devastating was the

TABLE 1
War-Related Deaths over the Centuries

Century	War Deaths (million)	Deaths per 1,000 people
1st to 15th	3.7	n.a.
16th	1.6	3.2
17th	6.1	11.2
18th	7.0	9.7
19th	19.4	16.2
20th	109.7[1]	44.4

[1] Up to 1995.
Source: See endnote 12.

enormous size of the armies that were mobilized. Universal conscription, first introduced in Prussia in 1814, had become the rule in most major military powers by the end of the nineteenth century, making large, permanent armies possible. Railways and the telegraph, key mid-century inventions, revolutionized war logistics and permitted huge armies to be transported over long distances. Some 20 million Europeans were sent off to fight in August 1914, and by 1918 a total of 65 million soldiers had been mobilized on all sides. Whereas

TABLE 2

Death Toll of Selected Wars, 1500–1945

Conflict	Time Period	Number Killed (thousand)	Civilian Victims (percent)
Peasants' War (Germany)	1524–1525	175	57
Dutch Independence War (vs. Spain)	1585–1604	177	32
30-Year War (Europe)	1618–1648	4,000	50
Spanish Succession War (Europe)	1701–1714	1,251	n.a.
7-Year War (Europe, North America, India)	1755–1763	1,358	27
French Revolutionary and Napoleonic wars	1792–1815	4,899	41
Crimean War (Russia, France, Britain)	1854–1856	772	66
U.S. Civil War	1861–1865	820	24
Paraguay vs. Brazil and Argentina	1864–1870	1,100	73
Franco-Prussian War	1870–1871	250	25
U.S.-Spanish War	1898	200	95
World War I	1914–1918	26,000	50
World War II	1939–1945	53,547	60

Source: See endnote 13.

just 1 percent of Europe's population was pulled into the fighting at the time of the Napoleonic Wars, 14 percent were called up in World War I. No society in human history had ever put forth as many soldiers, in absolute numbers and relative to total population, as Europe in 1914.[14]

And soldiers in the twentieth century were armed far more formidably than their predecessors. Rifles and cannons delivered greater punch over longer distances. War planes, tanks, and mass-produced chemical weapons were all added to World War I armories. All belligerents combined produced some 206,000 military airplanes during the war. British historian Eric Hobsbawm points out that Napoleon's victory over Prussia in the battle at Jena in 1806 was accomplished with 1,500 rounds of artillery. By comparison, France produced 200,000 shells *per day* during World War I (and still, like the other combatants, found these quantities to be inadequate). All told, the daily consumption of artillery shells by the leading powers increased 50-fold over the course of the war.[15]

Commenting on the old dictum that war is the continuation of politics by other means, military historian Martin van Crefeld has observed that "far from 'using' war as its instrument, the state now threatened to be devoured by it, people, economy, politics, government, and all." The war caused such a sharp drop in European living standards that it was not until 1924 that Western Europe regained the level of wealth it had attained before the war.[16]

Presumably, the horrors of World War I would have been sufficient to set the twentieth century on a different path, but the 1919 Treaty of Versailles prevented reconciliation. Instead, the punitive peace imposed on Germany strengthened revanchist forces there. Equally important, the Great Depression of 1929–1933 hit the global economy even harder than World War I had done. Trade and capital markets collapsed, and many countries, desperately attempting to extricate themselves from the slump, engaged in *beggar-thy-neighbor* policies—erecting trade barriers and engaging in competitive currency devaluations. Mass unemployment and ensuing hardships strained relations among countries and played an important role in the rise of fascism and the outbreak of World War II. In a sense, the entire period of 1914–1945 was one dominated by war.[17]

World War II dwarfed World War I in scale and, even more than the first global conflagration did, signaled a new era of warfare. It initiated total war—first, by being waged not just against military forces, but against a country's economy, infrastructure, and civilian population; and second, by mobilizing an unprecedented, massive portion of society's resources. Spurred by military demand, world aluminum production, for instance, which had heretofore been slated primarily for civilian use, doubled during World War I and nearly tripled during World War II, to satisfy the massive increases in the output of motor vehicles, warplanes, and engines.[18]

The warring states devoted the lion's share of their industrial strength and economic wealth to the all-or-nothing struggle that World War II became. The armed forces on all sides reached a peak level of 69 million soldiers. At least another 45 million persons were drawn into arms manufacturing, so that between one third and one half of the combatants' labor forces were directly or indirectly involved in the war effort. (See Table 3.)[19]

The major combatants (the United States, the Soviet Union, Germany, Britain, and Japan) produced armaments in awesome quantities, including at least 220,000 tanks and 840,000 aircraft.[20]

Soviet arms production increased 2.5-fold in 1940–1944, but civilian output suffered and agricultural production was cut in half. One quarter of the Soviet Union's prewar capital assets were destroyed, compared with 13 percent in Germany, and 7–8 percent in France and Italy. Britain had to liquidate almost its entire oversees holdings of capital in order to finance its war effort; it took the country several decades to restore its foreign investment position.[21]

Statistics about the human impact of World War II are numbing, so immense is the scale. An estimated 54 million people—soldiers and civilians—fell victim to front-line fight-

TABLE 3

Share of Working Population and Economy Devoted to War Effort, 1943–44

	Share of Working Population			
	Arms Industry	Armed Forces	Combined	Share of National Income (percent)
Soviet Union	31	23	54	76
United Kingdom	23	22	45	57
Germany	14	23	38[1]	76
United States	19	16	35	47

Source: See endnote 20.

ing, aerial bombardment, concentration camp mass murders, repression of uprisings, and disease and hunger. War deaths claimed an extraordinary 10–20 percent of the total population in the USSR, Poland, and Yugoslavia; 4–6 percent in Germany, Italy, Japan, and China; and about 1 percent in Britain, France, and the United States. World War I had generated about 4–5 million refugees. At the end of World War II, by comparison, an estimated 40 million people were uprooted in Europe alone—not including 11 million foreign forced laborers stranded in Germany or 14 million Germans expelled from eastern Europe. In Asia, the Japanese occupation of China left about 50 million Chinese homeless.[22]

The final acts of hostility of World War II—the dropping of atomic bombs over Hiroshima and Nagasaki—also heralded the beginning of the nuclear age and the coming Cold War. Huge quantities of resources were devoted to developing, building, and maintaining nuclear arsenals— weapons far more powerful than all the weapons built throughout human history combined. The United States alone spent at least $5.5 trillion (in 1996 dollars). How much the Soviet Union and the other nuclear powers poured out may never be known.[23]

With the help of 2,051 test explosions, the United States, the Soviet Union, and the smaller nuclear-weapons states developed and deployed huge armaments. (See Figure 1.) The global stockpile peaked at 69,000 nuclear warheads in 1986, containing an explosive yield of 18 billion tons of TNT, or 3.6 tons for every human being. In comparison, "only" 6 million tons of explosive force were used in World War II.[24]

Though overshadowed by the nuclear arsenals, the firepower, speed, range, and maneuverability of conventional weapons have soared as well. Governments have developed a dizzying variety of weapons. For instance, some 650 different kinds of missiles have been deployed worldwide during the past half century, with increasing targeting accuracy. But if the technical sophistication of weapons systems has escalated, so have the costs of relentless military innovation. Compared with World War II-era tanks, those of the early to mid-1990s cost 88 times as much per unit; bombers cost 130 times as much, and fighter airplanes almost 2,000 times as much.[25]

Governments have lavished funds on research and

FIGURE 1

Global Nuclear Weapons Stockpiles, 1945–97

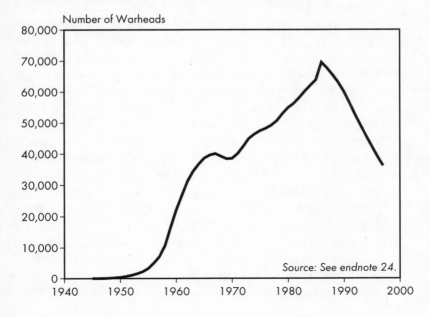

Source: See endnote 24.

development to produce technical breakthroughs for the military. Global military R&D spending reached a peak of approximately $124 billion in 1988 (but has since declined to $73 billion in 1993). Extrapolating from U.S. data, cumulative worldwide resources devoted to military innovation amounted to some $3.5 trillion during the past half century.[26]

Developing and buying weapons and maintaining large armies have had their costs. Estimates of military expenditures during World War I range from $1.4 trillion to $2.5 trillion (in 1998 dollars). The early interwar years saw a brief respite; but in the 1930s, world military spending increased from about $50–60 billion per year to about $150 billion on the eve of World War II. Outlays during that conflict may have come to at least $6 trillion, or up to about $1 trillion per year. Hence, global military expenditures toward the end of the Cold War—peaking at roughly $1.3 trillion per year in the late 1980s—not only rivaled total World War I expenditures but actually surpassed the annual spending during the largest war in human history.[27]

While the superpowers and their main allies were arming themselves for a doomsday standoff, they also spread arms in unprecedented quantity and quality across the planet. Since 1960, the global arms trade amounted to at least $1.5 trillion. Of that total, the majority—perhaps as much as two thirds—went to developing countries, often indebting the recipients and skewing their national budget priorities. In the 12-year period of 1984–1995 alone, for instance, the developing world received about 15,000 tanks; 34,000 artillery pieces; 27,000 armored personnel carriers and armored cars; close to 1,000 warships and submarines; 4,200 combat aircraft; more than 3,000 helicopters; some 48,000 missiles; and probably millions of small-caliber arms.[28]

This massive infusion of arms helped destabilize countries and regions that were in the throes of anti-colonial struggles, ethnic rivalries, and numerous other unresolved conflicts. It is little wonder, then, that the number of armed conflicts in the post-World War II era surged. (See Figure 2.) No single one of these wars could measure up to the earlier world wars, but together they have killed almost as many people as died during World War I. Some of them were incredibly destructive, considering that individually they affected limited territories and populations; Korea lost 10 percent of its population to war in the early 1950s, and Vietnam lost 13 percent in the 1960s and 1970s. (See Table 4.)[29]

Most wars since 1945 have been internal conflicts. Between 1989 and 1997, only 6 out of 103 armed conflicts were international. And the share of civilians among the victims has risen to ever higher levels: perhaps 70 percent of all war casualties since World War II, but more than 90 percent in the 1990s.[30]

The fact that almost all contemporary violent conflicts are internal wars does not mean that they have no wider dimension of concern to the international community.

TABLE 4

Largest Armed Conflicts since 1945[1]

Conflict	Time Period	Number Killed (thousand)	Civilian Victims (percent)
China (civil war)	1946–50	1,000	50
North v. South Korea (international intervention)	1950–53	3,000	50
North v. South Vietnam (U.S. intervention)	1960–75	2,358	58
Nigeria (Biafra civil war)	1967–70	2,000	50
Cambodia (civil war & foreign intervention)	1970–89	1,221	69
Bangladesh (secession from Pakistan)	1971	1,000	50
Afghanistan (Soviet intervention)	1978–92	1,500	67
Mozambican civil war	1981–94	1,050	95
Sudan (civil war)	1984 onward	1,500[2]	97

[1]Conflicts that killed 1 million persons or more. [2]Numbers up to 1995 only; the conflict continues today.
Source: See endnote 29.

Armed Conflicts, 1945–98

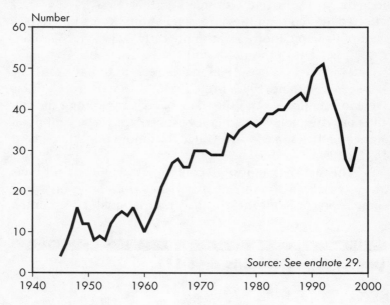

Source: See endnote 29.

Apart from foreign intervention in some cases, there are a variety of connections among internal wars within a region. For example, the civil wars in Rwanda and Burundi of the 1990s mutually influenced each other to some degree; and the Rwandan genocide of 1994 had a powerful spillover effect on the former Zaire, including the overthrow of the Mobutu dictatorship and, since then, insurrection against the ensuing Kabila regime that has drawn six neighboring countries into the fray.[31]

The twentieth century thus presents us with a paradox. It represents the culmination of a process begun some 350 years ago, in which states have become ever more powerful, investing enormous resources in sophisticated weapons, establishing large standing armies, and in the process building up relentlessly toward ever higher levels of organized violence. Yet with the end of the Cold War, this buildup reached its denouement: violence *between* sovereign states, though not unthinkable, has become less likely and far less frequent, whereas violence *within* societies has become commonplace. Yet security policy appears to be largely impervious to these changes, in two ways. One, the arsenals of many governments, and particularly those of the most advanced countries, are still brimming with tanks, jet fighters, naval destroyers, and missiles designed for a major war. More fundamentally, governments cling to the belief that there can be simple military solutions to complex social, economic, and environmental challenges. Altering these perceptions and assumptions will be a critical task in the twenty-first century.

Peace and Disarmament in the Twentieth Century

In his early seventeenth century treatise, *The Law of War and Peace*, Dutch scholar Hugo Grotius lamented, "I observed everywhere in Christendom a lawlessness in warfare of which even barbarous nations would be ashamed." Throughout history, human societies have made efforts to civilize warfare, though, as Grotius suggests, they met with limited success. Governments have sought to promote the rule of law in international relations; provide for avenues of peaceful settlement of conflicts; impose stricter rules governing the conduct of war (codifying the expected behavior of combatants toward each other, specifying the need to spare non-combatants, and trying to limit the "unnecessary suffering" that weapons are capable of inflicting); and create institutions for the common good. If the twenty-first century is to become an age of peace, we will need to keep refining and strengthening the tools that the twentieth century has given us.[32]

As the power of states to wield military force and to inflict widespread destruction mounted, the so-called civilizing endeavors became more critical. From the mid-nine-teenth century on, efforts were made to delineate war rules in international conventions. The two Hague peace conferences of 1899 and 1907 greatly advanced the development of such rules by codifying what had heretofore been verbal under-standings or inconsistently applied ideas. The Hague Conventions that emerged spell out norms for the treatment of prisoners of war, civilians, and victims of warfare. More agreements followed—all in all, some 41 international humanitarian laws are currently in force. (See Table 5.)[33]

To a large extent, the rule-writing has been an effort to catch up with realities, such as new means of waging war and the changing nature of conflicts. The 1977 Environmental Modification Convention, for instance, instructs states not to engage in any military use of environmental modification techniques that have "widespread, long-lasting or severe effects," and defines these techniques as "the deliberate manipulation of natural processes—the dynamics, composi-tion or structure of the Earth, including its biota, lithos-phere, hydrosphere and atmosphere, or ... outer space." Whereas war laws had traditionally covered interstate wars, the Second Protocol Additional to the 1949 Geneva Con-ventions, adopted in 1977, sought to address the protection of victims in *internal* conflicts, in recognition that such con-flicts have become the dominant forms of war in our time.[34]

Efforts to civilize warfare have clearly had some success; nonetheless, they have frequently, and perhaps inevitably, run into the reality of war's intrinsic savagery. One reason is that the indiscriminate killing power of many modern weapons is simply not susceptible to fine distinctions drawn up on paper. Secondly, the usefulness of weapons to the mil-itary has typically prevailed over the public interest in judg-ing whether particular weapons and weapons technologies should be permitted or outlawed. The military has been quite successful in warding off stronger norms, particularly concerning rules for internal wars. Thirdly, today's war laws allow the "incidental loss of civilian life"—a term that gives considerable latitude of interpretation. (For example, at a

U.N. war crimes tribunal in early 1999, the Pentagon argued that indiscriminate shelling of Serb civilians by Croatia in 1995—whose army received advice from retired U.S. generals—constituted legitimate military activity, even though tribunal investigators are calling for the indictment of the Croatian commanders.) Finally, the warlords and other non-state protagonists of today's fighting typically disregard existing war law; in fact, sowing terror among civilians appears to be one of their favorite tactics.[35]

More critical than war laws, however, is the advocacy of human rights, which blossomed in the twentieth century. The advancement of human rights—initially focused on civil and political rights, and followed by so-called second-generation (economic, social, and cultural) and third-generation rights (rights to development, peace, and a decent environment)—implicitly annuls war as a legitimate tool, since warfare denies the enjoyment of these rights. The 1968 Teheran Human Rights Conference stated this principle unambiguously: "Peace is the underlying condition for the full observance of human rights and war is their negation."[36]

Today there are more than 70 international and regional conventions, agreements, and declarations on human rights. Although many countries still have not signed and ratified these legal instruments, and even though the standing of human rights in large parts of the world has a long way to go before they amount to more than an assertion of liberties, there can be no doubt that human rights advocacy has been one of the most transformative factors of our age. In an age of rising internal warfare, when good governance and accountability are key to reducing the potential for violent conflict, human rights assume an ever more critical role: where they are respected—that is, where individuals are allowed to freely associate, express their opinions, and organize into groups and parties—there is usually sufficient political space for civil society to resolve disputes and cope with challenges.[37]

Prior to the twentieth century, recourse to force was seen as the sovereign right of governments. But the experi-

TABLE 5

Major Humanitarian, Human Rights, and Arms Control Treaties of the 20th Century

Humanitarian/ Laws of War	Human Rights	Arms Control/ Disarmament
1907 Hague Conventions	1948 Universal Declaration of Human Rights	1959 Antarctic Treaty
1925 Protocol Prohibiting Use of Poison Gas	1951 Convention Relating to the Status of Refugees	1967 Outer Space Treaty
1929 Geneva Conventions	1966 Covenant on Economic, Social, and Cultural Rights	1969/1995 Nuclear Non-Proliferation Treaty
1948 Genocide Convention	1966 Covenant on Civil and Political Rights	1971 Seabed Treaty
1949 Geneva Convention	1984 Anti-Torture Convention	1972 Biological Weapons Convention
1976 Environmental Modification Convention		1993 Chemical Weapons Convention
1977 Protocols Additional to 1949 Geneva Convention		1996 Nuclear Test-Ban Treaty
1980/1995 Inhumane Weapons Convention		1997 Anti-Personnel Landmine Convention

Source: See endnote 33.

ence of total, uninhibited, global warfare in the twentieth century underscores the fact that efforts confined to regulating conduct only during war are sorely inadequate. In order to survive, humanity needs international norms precluding the use of force in the first place. It is one of the accomplishments of the twentieth century—though one still being violated—that the use of force is now considered illegal except in self-defense. The U.N. Charter states unambiguously that "all Members shall refrain in their international relations from the threat or use of force against the territorial integrity or political independence of any state ..." The use of force within a country's borders, too, is less and less seen as acceptable, though governmental opinions on this matter diverge widely, and the international community has shown itself to be highly selective in addressing the issue (and thus, we witness intervention in Iraq but not in Turkey or Tibet, and in Kosovo but not in Chechnya or East Timor).[38]

An important part of the efforts to limit the use of force has been the creation of international organizations through which states could discuss their affairs and settle their differences peacefully. Reflecting the growing complexity of human society, such organizations have proliferated in the twentieth century: global organizations with broad mandates (such as the League of Nations and the United Nations); regional organizations (such as the European Union, Organization of American States, Organization of African Unity, and Association of Southeast Asian Nations); financial institutions (such as the International Monetary Fund and World Bank); and specialized agencies (such as the International Atomic Energy Agency or the World Meteorological Organization). All told, intergovernmental organizations mushroomed from just 37 in 1909 to 154 in 1960 and to more than 400 by 1997.[39]

The most representative and broadly constituted body is the United Nations, whose membership grew from an original 51 states in 1945 to 185 today. Established "to save succeeding generations from the scourge of war," as the famous passage from the U.N. Charter puts it, much of the peace and security machinery of the United Nations was deadlocked by the Cold War; the veto power accorded the five so-called permanent members of the Security Council (whose self-bestowed privilege reflected the outcome of World War II and was forced on the other members) meant that the

Council was largely frozen into inactivity. With the end of the Cold War, however, the Council entered a period of frenzied activity. The number of resolutions, official statements, and consultations skyrocketed. Whereas from the late 1960s to the late 1980s, an average of 26 percent of all Council resolutions had been vetoed, in 1997 fewer than 6 percent met that fate.[40]

Forced by Cold War strictures to improvise, the United Nations came up with an important innovation when it invented peacekeeping—the dispatch of unarmed or lightly armed U.N. personnel to trouble spots. Initially their orders were to help patrol tense border areas and monitor ceasefire lines. Later, from the late 1980s on, they sought to supervise the implementation of complex peace treaties, including such tasks as disarming and demobilizing combatants and monitoring elections and human rights violations. During its first four decades, peacekeeping was very limited. Then, in the 1990s, it underwent a sudden spasm of growth: by 1994, the number of missions had jumped to 17, the ranks of peacekeepers swelled to almost 80,000, and annual expenditures surpassed $3.3 billion.[41]

Still, the 1990s also underlined the fact that peacekeeping operations were run on an ad hoc basis, that the U.N. was responding to crises by hastily cobbling together missions from national contingents that brought with them sharply divergent levels of training and equipment as well as sometimes incompatible philosophies and varying degrees of political commitment. Financing—both for peacekeeping and for the organization as a whole—has been highly unstable, with the United States in particular running up debts that threaten to cripple the U.N.[42]

Moreover, following substantial difficulties in Somalia and Bosnia, key members of the Security Council quickly became disenchanted with peacekeeping. U.N. involvement in conflict resolution was scaled back dramatically. Some missions were phased out or scaled down prematurely, before they fully accomplished the task of re-establishing peace; in some conflicts, the Council refused to get involved at all. By the end of 1998, fewer than 15,000 peacekeepers were in the field, and expenditures had retreated to less than $1 billion. The United States now increasingly prefers to have either NATO- or U.S.-led ad hoc coalitions run peace-keeping operations, particularly when it appears that other permanent members of the Security Council may block U.S. policies. As a result, the U.N. is once again being sidelined in matters of international peace and security.[43]

While the U.N.'s involvement in military and security matters remained limited throughout the Cold War years and is now again in question, it has been clear from the first days of the organization that many of its other activities—from promoting anti-poverty and child survival programs to assisting education efforts, advocating women's rights, encouraging fair elections and human rights adherence, and promoting sustainable development—have a significant bearing on peace. These activities draw

True peace ... requires justice and equity.

support from the recognition that true peace depends on more than the guns falling silent; it requires justice and equity, and a sufficient degree of human well-being.

When the Food and Agriculture Organisation was set up, its task of improving nutritional standards was expressly understood as a contribution to economic and political stability and hence to the prevention of future wars. The UNESCO charter states that "since wars begin in the minds of men, it is in the minds of men that the defenses of peace must be constructed." Meanwhile, the Preamble to the constitution of the International Labour Organisation (ILO) notes that injustice generates "unrest so great that the peace and harmony of the world are imperiled." It should come as no surprise that U.N. agencies and officials have been awarded a total of 11 Nobel Peace prizes. Only one of these prizes went to the U.N. peacekeeping forces, in 1988; others were awarded to the U.N. High Commissioner for Refugees (in 1954 and 1981), U.N. Secretary-General Dag Hammarskjöld (1961), UNICEF (1965), and the ILO (1969).[44]

As part of the United Nations system, the World Court was established as a forum to which nations could turn for peaceful settlement of their disputes—the culmination of 200 years of efforts to institutionalize international arbitration. Disputes can be brought before the court in one of three ways. First, several hundred international economic, arms control, environmental, and other treaties give it jurisdiction to iron out differences in interpretation (among them are, for instance, the Chemical Weapons Convention, the Genocide Convention, and the Convention Relating to the Status of Refugees, the Framework Convention on Climate Change, and the Convention on Biological Diversity). Second, countries may agree bilaterally to submit an existing dispute. Third, states may decide to generally accept the court's compulsory jurisdiction. But only a relatively small number of nations (59 by 1996) have accepted this latter role for the court. Moreover, 41 of them have conditioned or limited their consent, and another 12 countries, the United States among them, have withdrawn their earlier consent.[45]

Although the court has enjoyed a significant rise in the number of disputes brought before it since 1986, on the whole it remains sorely underused: it has so far delivered 61 judgments in response to a total of 74 cases considered, and it has rendered a total of 23 advisory opinions. Cases actually brought before it have often involved minor matters instead of the kind of high-profile issues that could establish the court as a key organ in regulating international affairs. Thus, the World Court's current role in the peaceful settlement of conflicts is still far from matching its potential.[46]

Near the close of the twentieth century, the international community is also belatedly making progress on a related matter: the establishment of an International Criminal Court (ICC). This is, in a sense, the crowning event of a long struggle concerning the conduct of warfare and the legality of war itself. In 1919, attempts to prosecute crimes committed during World War I were unsuccessful. In 1946, the victors of World War II established an International

Military Tribunal to prosecute Nazi leaders for crimes against peace (that is, waging a war of aggression), war crimes (violating accepted norms limiting the conduct of war), and crimes against humanity (genocide and other systematic and widespread persecutions of civilian populations). But the Cold War rivalry prevented establishment of a permanent court and allowed countless cases of aggression, genocide, and atrocities against civilian populations. Only the end of the Cold War permitted the adoption of even a stop-gap measure: the creation of ad hoc tribunals, in 1993 and 1994, for the former Yugoslavia and Rwanda.[47]

The changed international climate following the Cold War permitted resumption of work on setting up a permanent court, leading to a conference in July 1998 at which governments voted to establish an international criminal court. (Although the vote was 120 in favor to seven against, with 21 abstentions, at least 60 countries will have to ratify the treaty before it enters into force; 78 states had signed the convention as of mid-March 1999, but only one had ratified it.) The court's independence and effectiveness were contentious issues, and the key question for supporters of a strong ICC was how far to compromise in order to finally gain the institution whose creation had proved elusive for so long. (See Table 6.) To the distress of many, the United States fought for a very restricted and weak court and in the end voted against its creation.[48]

Disarmament was on the agenda of the 1899 Hague conference. But at that gathering and during the first half of the twentieth century, governments merely talked about disarmament without ever achieving it. During the Cold War, the world had to content itself with a limited number of weak arms control measures that did little to restrain the dynamic of the arms race. The end of the East-West confrontation—and of several hot wars—has permitted the world to climb down from the extreme heights of overkill arsenals.

Military expenditures have declined by some 40 percent from their mid-1980s peak—a decline surpassed in magnitude only in the years immediately following World Wars I and II. The ranks of the armed forces have been trimmed by almost 6 million soldiers, or about 20 percent, from the 1988 peak level of 28.7 million. The number of military bases and soldiers stationed on foreign soils has also declined substantially, from some 2 million in the late 1980s to about 500,000 by the mid-1990s. Worldwide, holdings of tanks and armored vehicles, artillery, combat aircraft, and major fighting ships have fallen about 31 percent between 1990 and 1996, although the experience from region to region varies. The conventional arms trade, running amok in the 1980s, took a nosedive in the 1990s. From a peak of $84.4 billion in 1987 (in 1996 dollars), the value of weapons transfers fell to less than $38.5 billion in 1994. But since then, governmental and corporate arms peddlers have managed to halt this promising trend: in 1996, the most recent year for which data are available, arms sales reached an estimated $42.6 billion.[49]

Nuclear arsenals, too, have been trimmed, from close to 70,000 warheads to about 36,000 by 1997. But the equivalent of 8 billion tons of TNT concentrated in these weapons is still far more than is required to destroy the entire planet. Four nations actually relinquished their nuclear arms: Belarus, Kazakhstan, and Ukraine transferred the arsenals they inherited from the Soviet Union to Russia, and South Africa dismantled warheads as the apartheid regime came to an end. Yet India and Pakistan affirmed their quest for nuclear status by setting off several test explosions, while Israel continues to be a de facto nuclear power.[50]

The post-Cold War reduction in conventional and nuclear forces is best seen as merely a thinning out of arsenals—akin to pruning badly overgrown weeds. The Chemical Weapons Convention (CWC) is one of the few instances in which a whole class of weapons has actually been outlawed and disarmament realized. (The Biological Weapons Convention, too, entails similar prohibitions, but because there are no verification or enforcement mechanisms, the treaty is widely regarded as ineffective.)

Attempts to ban the development or use of various

types of poison weapons date back at least to the seventeenth century, but such efforts did not prevent the large-scale use of chemical weapons during World War I—when 66 million artillery shells were fired off to disperse 124,000 tons of chemical agents, killing and wounding 1 million people. The ensuing public outrage compelled governments to agree to the 1925 Geneva Protocol, which banned the use of chemical weapons but failed to proscribe their production and stockpiling. Following many years of negotiations, the CWC was opened for signature in 1993 and entered into force in April 1997; it has so far been signed by 169 states. The convention forbids the development, production, trade, possession, and use of chemical warfare agents and mandates that existing stockpiles and production facilities be eliminated.[51]

War may have reached the ultimate scale in our century, and peace may never have been a more existential condition for human survival, but musings about war and peace are nothing new. All through human history, one finds lofty rhetoric about peace, realism about the terrible impact of warfare, and skepticism about war's merits. What is different in our age is that civil society—peace movements and other citizens' groups—appears to be playing a far more important role than in the past, trying to subject security policy to greater public scrutiny and to wrest it from the narrow control of military bureaucracies and defense intellectuals.[52]

As the destructive power of weaponry accelerated with the Industrial Revolution, the quest for peace became more urgent. Local and national peace societies were founded in Europe throughout the nineteenth century, although the earliest such groups appeared in the United States (New York in 1815) and in Britain. By 1886 there were some 36 peace societies. International contacts and coordination grew and improved with initiation of annual World Peace Congresses in 1889 and the establishment of the International Peace Bureau in Bern in 1892.[53]

The early peace movements, like those of our day, were affected by the ebb and flow of popular interest and support.

TABLE 6

Advantages and Drawbacks of the New International Criminal Court

Advantages	Drawbacks
Court has jurisdiction over genocide, crimes against humanity, and war crimes.	States can reject the court's jurisdiction over war crimes for the first seven years.
Aggression is included as a core crime.	A legal definition of aggression has yet to be agreed to.
Court has jurisdiction over crimes committed in international and internal wars.	The list of prosecutable crimes for internal conflicts is limited (does not include forced starvation or gassing of civilians).
Court can initiate investigations, based on information from victims, NGOs, or any other reliable source.	Court cannot act unless the state of the accused person's nationality or the state where the crimes took place have ratified the treaty.
The U.N. Security Council does not have a veto over the ICC's proceedings.	The Council, if unanimous, can request a one-year delay of prosecution and renew the request indefinitely, in one-year segments.
States are required to comply with the Court's requests for cooperation.	States can withhold cooperation on national security grounds.
Civilian and military commanders can be held responsible for crimes of their subordinates.	There is a limited right to assert the existence of orders from one's superior as a defense.
Ratifying states cannot create reservations (by declaring that certain portions do not apply to them).	
Court can prosecute as war crimes the use of children under 15 as soldiers, rape, sexual slavery, or enforced pregnancy.	

Source: See endnote 48.

In 1891, Bertha von Suttner and her fellow activists watched public concern surge, only to see it fall off rapidly in the following year. In the twentieth century, millions of people were mobilized against nuclear war in the 1950s and 1960s, but as the politics of détente seemed to diminish the danger, the public's attention shifted elsewhere; the same scenario played itself out in the 1980s and 1990s, when the Cold War first intensified and then came to an end.

Seemingly heralding an age of peace, the end of the East-West standoff has made it difficult to rally public opinion on issues of peace and disarmament. At the same time, however, the involvement of a broad variety of nongovernmental organizations (NGOs) has expanded the traditional peace agenda. In the 1980s, Western peace groups were consumed by narrow, weapons-focused questions such as the hair-trigger alert of nuclear strike forces and "circular-error probability"—a measure of how precisely intercontinental missiles could be targeted.

Now, NGOs that are concerned with such varied issues as human rights, governmental transparency and accountability, environmental protection, human development, and justice and equity increasingly weigh in on matters of peace and war as well, reflecting a broadened understanding of the preconditions for peace and injecting a new dynamic. For instance, the successful campaigns against anti-personnel landmines and for the International Criminal Court were spearheaded not by traditional arms control groups, but by human rights organizations and groups with social and humanitarian agendas. The same is true for the "World Court Project"—a successful effort to get the World Court to render an advisory opinion on the legality of nuclear weapons (the Court ruled in 1996 that the threat or use of nuclear weapons would generally violate international law, and that there is a legal obligation to conclude negotiations toward the abolition of nuclear arms).[54]

Recognizing the global nature of many contemporary challenges, many NGOs are no longer active only within the borders of their own countries. The twentieth century, particularly its second half, has witnessed a proliferation not only of NGOs in general, but also of international groups (defined as operating in at least three countries). In 1909, they numbered just 176, but their ranks rose to at least 985 in 1956, reaching more than 20,000 by 1996. The number of NGOs that are formally accredited to cooperate and consult with the U.N. Economic and Social Council rose from 41 in 1948 to more than 1,500 in 1998. Clearly, they play an increasingly visible and active role in shaping international affairs.[55]

Through the NGOs, civil society's influence is without doubt far greater than in the days of Bertha von Suttner, when she, and other peace activists, were barred from attending the sessions of the 1899 Hague Peace Conference. The hard work of those activists who lobbied participating governments provided a foundation for the active involvement of NGOs that we now take for granted. Today, legions of NGO representatives can be found at important international gatherings, and often there are even NGO conferences paralleling official ones. Because they bring social, environmental, and humanitarian perspectives, not military-strategic considerations, to the fore, civil-society organizations hold considerable hope for a new peace and security policy in the future.

Still, the rise of NGOs does prompt a host of new questions. As one recent observer, P.J. Simmons of the Carnegie Endowment for International Peace, argued: "Embracing a bewildering array of beliefs, interests, and agendas, they have the potential to do as much harm as good. Hailed as exemplars of grassroots democracy in action, many NGOs are, in fact, decidedly undemocratic and unaccountable to the people they claim to present." While NGOs have, on the whole, played a democratizing role in international affairs, the issue of how representative, democratic, and accountable these groups are becomes increasingly important as their success mounts. This may be one of the contradictions of making international relations more open, but it is well to remember Winston Churchill's observation that democracy is the worst form of government except for all the other forms that have been tried from time to time.[56]

The Roots of Today's Conflicts

Concluding a process set in motion with the 1648 Treaty of Westphalia, nation states reached the pinnacle of their power in the twentieth century. During these 350 years, central governments concentrated on securing for them-selves sovereign rights such as exercising supreme authority over their national territories, collecting taxes, and waging war abroad. Within their borders, governments imposed a monopoly on the use of violence. In return, they were expected to protect their citizens. And to the extent that they managed to provide for their populations' well-being and slowly became more democratic and accountable, they gained legitimacy. The rise of nationalism in the nineteenth and twentieth centuries cemented and enhanced central governments' position.

State power and state violence converged to a zenith in the two world wars. Never before or since were such gargan-tuan armies raised. Never before or since was total war waged. Governments marshaled unprecedented resources for their arms industries. They took "a hand in everything con-sidered even remotely relevant to the war effort," as Prof. van Crefeld observes. "This included people's health, their living conditions, their calorie intake, their wages, their profes-sional qualifications, their freedom of movement, and so on ad infinitum."[57]

While the potential of renewed big-power confronta-tion cannot be excluded, other concerns have risen to the top of the global agenda. Although governments continued to pour enormous resources into the military after 1945, two critical changes were in the making. Obscured at first by pre-occupation with the Cold War and nuclear weaponry, these changes are now becoming quite obvious.

The first is a shift from interstate war, waged by governments against one another, to internal wars and skirmishes. The fighting now is done as often by paramilitary forces, guerrilla groups, ethnic militias, vigilante squads, even criminal gangs, as by regular, uniformed soldiers. The distinction between combatants and non-combatants is often blurred, and these kinds of wars are just as rarely declared as they are ever formally terminated. Today, almost all armed conflicts are of this nature. (See Map.) The second change, discussed below in greater detail, is the emergence of the twin phenomena of localization and globalization. Both shifts threaten to undermine the pre-eminence in human affairs to which nation states had grown so accustomed over the past 350 years, and they therefore hold important implications for war and peace.[58]

Today's conflicts are typically not driven by great power rivalries, but rather by a multitude of pressures and instabilities that threaten to shred the social fabric of societies. A toxic brew of growing disparities in wealth, increasing unemployment and job insecurity, population growth, and environmental degradation is provoking more social discontent and polarization, leading to political strife in many countries and to devastating violence in some. Although developing countries are most affected and most vulnerable, richer industrial nations are by no means immune to some of the same stress factors.[59]

With the exception of global environmental degradation, these underlying factors are, of course, nothing new. In fact, even though extreme nationalism and imperial rivalries played an important role in pushing Europe toward war in 1914, social, economic, and ethnic fissures produced significant internal stress that contributed to belligerence. Strong population growth translated into rising land scarcity and brought village life and customs under enormous strain, as young people increasingly lacked the material basis for establishing a family. The social and economic transformations of rapid urbanization and industrialization brought additional pressures in cities. In eastern Europe, job creation fell far

short of burgeoning populations. Mass emigration—almost
18 million people left Europe for other continents between
1880 and 1914—provided only a partial safety valve. Ethnic
hatreds in the multinational Russian and Habsburg empires
ran rampant, as did anti-Semitism. As disparities in wealth
widened and the emerging labor and socialist movements
struggled for overdue economic and political change, class
antagonism soared.[60]

However, governments managed to contain these pressures; although civil strife occurred (particularly in Russia in
1905), historian William McNeill notes that the extreme
patriotism and nationalism of the age helped channel and
project antagonisms outward, toward external adversaries.
Today, by contrast, similar underlying pressures are more
likely to lead to the weakening and unraveling of states and
to internal warfare.[61]

Now the strains are making themselves felt clearly. In
recent decades, the gap between rich and poor has grown
dramatically. In 1960, those in the top 20 percent worldwide
had 30 times the income of those in the bottom 20 percent;
by the beginning of the 1990s, they had almost 60 times as
much. This gaping disparity is replicated within individual
countries, more severely in some than others. In the context
of globalization, the inequitable distribution of economic
opportunities and social burdens is becoming far more pro-
nounced. At the same time, modern information and communications channels ensure that awareness of these
disparities among people is much higher than in the past.[62]

Unemployment is already a worrisome phenomenon
practically everywhere in the world. Overall, at least 150 million people are out of work and another 900 million or so are
underemployed—involuntarily working less than full time
or earning less than a living wage. Altogether, one third of
the global labor force is un- or underemployed. And pressure
on labor markets is bound to intensify with strong population growth. Most future job seekers—96 percent of the more
than 700 million people who are expected to join the world's
economically active population between 1995 and 2010—

MAP

Countries in Armed Conflict, 1998

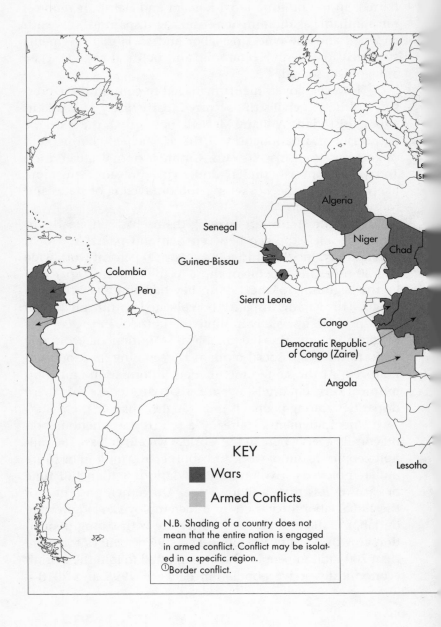

KEY

Wars

Armed Conflicts

N.B. Shading of a country does not mean that the entire nation is engaged in armed conflict. Conflict may be isolated in a specific region.
①Border conflict.

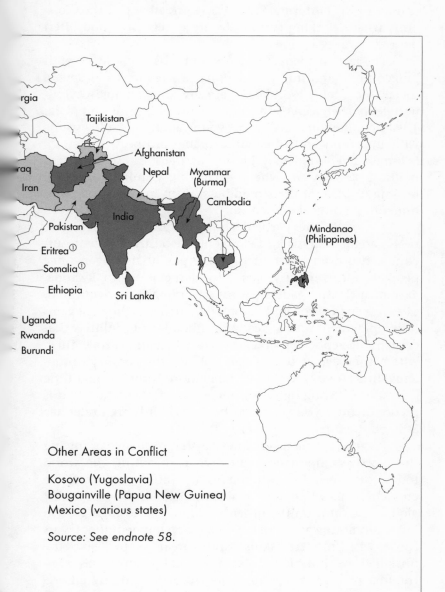

rgia

Tajikistan

Afghanistan

Nepal   Myanmar
(Burma)

raq

Iran   Cambodia

India

Mindanao
(Philippines)

Pakistan

Eritrea[1]

Somalia[1]

Ethiopia   Sri Lanka

Uganda
Rwanda
Burundi

Other Areas in Conflict

Kosovo (Yugoslavia)
Bougainville (Papua New Guinea)
Mexico (various states)

Source: See endnote 58.

will be citizens of developing countries. Strong urban population growth and a continued influx of people from the
countryside make jobs in cities scarce; many young people
end up in the "informal" sector, the underbelly of the economy, where working conditions are unregulated and often
poor and wages are low.[63]

The lack of adequate numbers of jobs in countries with
burgeoning youthful populations is creating widespread
social discontent. Worldwide, already an estimated 60 million people between the ages of 15 and 24 cannot find work.
The phenomenon of legions of young adults and adolescents
with uncertain and often unfavorable prospects for establishing a livelihood may be one of the greatest threats to
political stability anywhere—triggering criminal behavior,
feeding discontent that could burst open in street riots, and
fomenting political extremism.[64]

Although the particular circumstances of each case
need careful analysis and can generate vastly different outcomes, two examples underline the potential dangers once
people are driven to violence by desperation. In Rwanda,
extremist Hutu leaders recruited primarily uneducated,
unemployed youth—individuals who had little hope of gain-
ful employment and a steady livelihood—into militias that
carried out genocidal violence in 1994 against ethnic Tutsi,
whom they depicted as responsible for the country's problems. In Kosovo, the Kosovo Liberation Army has had little
difficulty enlisting fighters from among a population that is
predominantly young (more than two thirds are under age
30) and unemployed (70 percent).[65]

It is not clear if a system exists that is capable of solving
the massive employment problem confronting the world
today. State-centered economies are often not dynamic
enough to generate sufficient employment. The capitalist
global economy, on the other hand, may yield high growth
but is promoting a type of economic development that favors
those with modern skills—and threatens to leave the
unskilled behind. Rapid technological change has contributed to a growing gap in job security and pay among

workers with different skill levels. And as deregulation and privatization take hold in economy after economy, the imperative of global competitiveness seems to demand corporate "downsizing" and the elimination of public sector jobs.[66]

Unemployment, job insecurity, persistent poverty, and the growing divide between rich and poor have fueled social conflict across Latin America. A wrenching and uncertain economic transformation in the formerly Communist nations of Eastern Europe has led to a rapid emergence of mass unemployment and poverty there. And with its economy verging on collapse—gross national product has fallen by an estimated 50–80 percent during the 1990s—Russia may be a time bomb socially and politically. Finally, the Asian crisis has deprived at least 10 million people of their jobs in just one year. With few social protections in place, the result has been poverty and misery for many. As events in Indonesia suggest, spreading social suffering could lead to large-scale unrest.[67]

Environmentally induced conflict is far more likely within than between nations.

Equity issues also interact with growing resource scarcity and environmental degradation. The depletion of freshwater resources, excessive exploitation of fisheries, degradation of arable land, and deforestation, among other problems, not only affect human health and well-being and imperil the habitability of some regions, but they are also increasingly understood to play an important role in generating or exacerbating some conflicts. Although several transboundary environmental disputes exist and some of them could escalate in the future, environmentally induced conflict is far more likely within than between nations.[68]

Developing countries—particularly those whose economies are heavily geared toward agriculture and other sectors that directly depend on the health of the natural resource base—are most affected by environmental problems. There, the needs and interests of contending groups tied closely to the land—farmers, nomads, ranchers, and resource extractors—often are at odds and remain unreconciled. Conflicts over scarce land and water abound. As cases from Mexico, Nigeria, Sudan, Papua New Guinea, India, and other countries show, poorer communities, minority groups, and indigenous peoples typically bear the brunt of adverse environmental change, particularly that triggered by oil drilling, mining, logging, and large-scale dam and irrigation projects. There is now growing recognition of the environment-conflict linkage.[69]

If climate change becomes a full-blown reality, it will compound present environmental challenges by raising sea levels, shifting vegetation zones, and changing precipitation patterns. If heavily populated coastal areas are inundated and crop harvests in some regions are decimated by more frequent droughts, to cite just two possible consequences, there could be dramatic increases in food insecurity. A flood of environmental refugees—displaced residents of engulfed coastal areas and farmers compelled to abandon their parched lands—may find it difficult to start a new livelihood in already crowded cities and may even clash with unwelcoming host communities. It is obviously impossible to predict either the dynamics of such a scenario or how well societies will cope, but in all likelihood, such changes would translate into a sharp increase in human conflict.[70]

Even short of catastrophic climate change, many natural systems—such as croplands, forests, and freshwater sources—show signs of increasing stress. All other things being equal, continued population growth intensifies these pressures. Depending on the ways in which environmental transformation translates into the social, economic, and political realms, environmental decline could grow into an increasingly significant factor in violent disputes in coming decades. What matters most in this regard is not necessarily the hardships of environmental degradation per se, but rather that the harmful impacts will be felt highly unevenly by different social strata, communities, and countries. This uneven impact may well reinforce social and economic inequities and deepen patterns of polarization in society. For instance, the Sardar Sarovar dam and irrigation project in India's Narmada Valley will primarily benefit a small number of wealthy farmers, while the burdens—flooding of villages and arable land, decimation of local fisheries, and loss of ancestral land and cultural monuments—will fall on hundreds of thousands of poorer peasants.[71]

Where governments show themselves unable or unwilling to deal with these accelerating pressures, they stand to lose legitimacy, and people turn to the more immediate group or community they belong to in search of support, identity, and security. But individual groups in such situations often feel they are competing head-on against each other for scarce resources and services, and governments may even encourage such splits in classical divide-and-rule fashion. All too often, the end result is a polarization and splintering of societies, literally inviting violent responses to unresolved problems. Reacting to such problems, central governments may seek to impose authoritarian solutions. Or the society may unravel and collapse.

Although a substantial share of the responsibility for these conditions lies within individual countries, outside factors play an important role too. The first factor is the legacy of the Cold War. East-West geopolitics ascribed strategic value to certain parts of the developing world, mostly for reasons of resource endowment or geostrategic location; the industrialized countries accordingly intervened in a variety of ways and armed their protégés to the teeth. Once this confrontation ended, however, the importance of many once-indispensable allies vanished. "Hot" Cold War battlegrounds like Afghanistan, the Horn of Africa, or Central America were abruptly abandoned and reverted to backwater status. Recipients of aid and weapons from the North saw the flow of assistance dry up. (Over the past decade, total U.S. aid to El Salvador, for instance, fell from more than $500 million to $34 million per year.)[72]

Without big-power sponsorship propping them up, many Third World armies are fragmenting, often resembling tools of regional warlords or simply armed gangs that loot and extort. War-torn nations have not received any Marshall Plan-type assistance to rebuild and get back on their feet. Meanwhile, the legacy of Cold War policies—the easy availability of weapons, a pervasive culture of violence, and a stunted political system—makes fertile ground for violent and authoritarian responses to unresolved problems.[73]

The second factor is economic. Many developing countries were and are bound into the global economy as highly dependent sellers of raw materials or simple manufactured goods. As advanced industrial countries' economies become geared more toward information and communications technologies, these trading relations inevitably undergo structural change. Reduced demand for certain commodities translates into weaker, more volatile prices, a trend reinforced by the oversupply that results from the simultaneous attempt of many producer countries to boost their commodity exports. Between 1980 and 1997, the nonfuel commodity price index (based on 1990 constant dollars) fell from 174 to 107; the petroleum price index fell from 224 to 76 during the same period. Economies dependent on the revenues that a single commodity or a handful of them can fetch on the world market are naturally vulnerable to these changes. As painful social and economic adjustments must be made, benefits and burdens are typically distributed highly unequally among rich and poor, and internal contradictions are sharpened.[74]

A central characteristic of our time, the shift from interstate to intrastate conflict, needs to be understood in the broader context of globalization and localization. These two contradictory, yet intersecting trends have diminished the importance of territorial and national concepts. States continue to be important players, but they are increasingly challenged by footloose corporations operating across the planet, by local grassroots groups and international coalitions of NGOs, by the march of technology that is rapidly creating a wired, interconnected planet, and even by the slow progress in creating international organizations and strengthening international norms.

As trade and investment flows, travel and communications, and technology development draw nations deeper into the global economy, they tie individual countries' fates together ever more tightly. Since this process takes place in the context of extensive privatization and deregulation, it tends to enhance the influence and power of corporations at the expense of governments. At the same time, we see a re-dedication to local customs, loyalties, and identities, spurred by two factors: the first is a sense that national governments can be less and less relied upon to provide essential services, security, and a sense of place in the world; the second is growing trepidation about what the forces of globalization hold in store. While many localizing efforts are benign, it is clear that some flow from a xenophobia that gives rise to the internal violence discussed earlier.

The upshot is that peace and security are more complex and ambiguous objectives than the traditional lens of national security can encompass. For centuries, world affairs revolved around questions of which states had hegemonic power, which were declining, and how alliances among states shifted. Governments regarded military power as being of paramount importance (not infrequently, this turned out to be an erroneous assumption, as states engaged in imperial overstretch and neglected crucial social and economic issues). Today, it may seem as though the world has simply entered another episode in this age-old game—moving from a world bifurcated between two hostile superpowers to one in which the United States is the sole remaining superpower ("the indispensable nation" in U.S. Secretary of State Madeleine Albright's words).[75]

In truth, we no longer live in a state-centric world, whether in its unipolar, bipolar, or multipolar incarnation. The meaning of national borders is inevitably changed in an age where such boundaries can be, and are, traversed with ever greater ease. This does not mean that states are no longer relevant, just that they have to share the stage with international or regional entities. Sovereignty may be eroding, but it is still being strongly asserted.[76]

What prospects does globalization hold for matters of peace and security? As national economies become more and more integrated and as economic interests coincide less and less with national boundaries, will there still be a major role for national armed forces? It is tempting to conclude that an increasingly interdependent world will of necessity lead to growing global cooperation and that armed forces will become superfluous. This expectation is further reinforced by the dawning recognition that individual nations are unable to cope on their own with global challenges such as climate change or transboundary pollution.[77]

Can economic integration then be an antidote to violent conflict? Recognizing that beggar-thy-neighbor policies caused a severe global economic crisis at the end of the 1920s that helped lead to the outbreak of World War II, political leaders after 1945 saw economic integration as a key remedy. In Western Europe, economic links became so tight as to make peace infinitely more beneficial than the gains anyone could hope to derive from rupturing these links. In contrast with the time after World War I, Germany was fully integrated into the postwar order (and the Marshall Plan allowed it to rise up from the war's ashes rapidly). In the process, strong and competent institutions emerged to regulate relations among European nations and resolve disputes. Democratic governance and respect for human rights grew far stronger and more widespread than they ever had before. And social welfare programs ensured a high degree of human well-being, greatly reducing the likelihood that social discontent would trigger large-scale violent conflict at home.

Although globalization's challenge to traditional notions of territorial-based security may over time help to make military-centered concepts of security far less relevant, such an outcome is by no means guaranteed. Historical evidence alone recommends caution. The era leading up to World War I was in fact marked by a substantial degree of economic interchange (though not nearly as all-encompassing and deeply penetrating as in our age). Yet growing trade and capital flows per se did not guarantee world peace. Even the experience of the European Union suggests that a common market does not necessarily lead to a common political system. As Martin van Crefeld bluntly puts it: "A continent-wide community whose sole purpose in life is to increase per-capita income and the Gross National Product will hardly be able to count on people's undivided loyalty."[78]

There is indeed danger in relaxing efforts to achieve peace based on the expectation that the erosion of economic borders will inevitably lead to political integration far beyond national boundaries and melt away remaining enmities. And a sense of global community that could supplant entrenched national identities does not come about simply as a result of economic structures; it needs to be based on more than cold financial calculation and has to be carefully nurtured. It is no accident that proposals for ever freer trade and enhanced border controls against unwanted immigrants and refugees are taking place side by side. Economic integration may be an effective antidote to warfare between those industrially advanced states that are close to the commanding heights of the world economic system (and therefore most likely to benefit from it), but far less so between those who are at its periphery.

Global community does not come about simply as a result of economic structures.

Furthermore, globalization itself carries the potential for tension and conflict. When the fates of national economies are tied together closely in a global unregulated market, the ripple effects of economic trouble can be devastating—as developments in Asia are showing so clearly. Globalization proceeds even as international financial and economic institutions—the International Monetary Fund and the World Bank—lag behind in their ability to cope with its repercussions.[79]

Economic integration only works to advance peace if it brings gains to broad sections of society. Yet the benefits and burdens of globalization are distributed in spectacularly uneven fashion, heightening disparities between and within nations. Because it entails severe dislocation and social pain, and because it is experienced as a challenge to local control and democratic accountability, economic globalization tears at the very fabric of many societies. The turbulent changes inherent in globalization may well trigger a growing backlash of parochialism and xenophobia, a phenomenon that Prof. Benjamin Barber of Rutgers University has called "Jihad vs. McWorld."[80]

This new era, simply by attenuating the power of states, will not necessarily produce a more peaceful twenty-first century. Territorial contests and conflicts, and with them traditional wars, may largely become a thing of the past. But globalization does not remove the appeal that the use of force may hold for some, and new forms of conflict are not difficult to imagine.

Already, we confront a trend toward privatization of security and violence, with internal battles and skirmishes fought among an array of non-state groups. Virtually everywhere on the globe, a tremendous rise in non-state and security forces is taking place. Some of them are old-fashioned guerrilla forces; others are citizen or ethnic militias, armed criminal gangs, mercenaries, and security forces hired by private corporations. These groups multiply even as armies break apart in some countries, military forces become increasingly involved in a variety of domestic policing tasks in other countries, and police forces become progressively militarized in yet others.[81]

Fast-forward to the past: In one sense, this kind of privatization may mark a return to a phenomenon that was quite common in earlier centuries. For instance, in the sixteenth and early seventeenth centuries, war in Europe was "a form of capitalist enterprise" as van Crefeld puts it, and armies routinely consisted of mercenaries. During the seventeenth and eighteenth centuries, the British East India Company fielded its own troops, numbering in the thousands. By 1773, the company had grown so powerful and displayed so many trappings of sovereignty that the British parliament saw no choice but to pass a law to bring the firm under greater government control.[82]

Forging a Peaceful New Century

Peace and security policy in the twenty-first century will have to deal both with the lingering legacies of the twentieth century—unquestioning acceptance of huge accumulated arsenals and of the use of force as an arbiter of human conflict—and with new challenges as well, such as internal conflicts arising from social, economic, demographic, and environmental pressures. These problems are intertwined. While the particular causes of our century's wars and arms races may quickly become history, the leftover military equipment now makes for such ready availability of arms of all calibers, particularly small arms, that recourse to violent measures in future disputes is far too easy. To forestall the likelihood of endless skirmishes and wars in the coming century, governments, intergovernmental institutions, and civil society groups will need to find renewed vigor to pursue demilitarization, conflict prevention, more inspired global institution-building, and greater grassroots engagement.

During the Cold War years, the recognition grew that traditional security policies—building national or allied military muscle—often yielded insecurity. A series of independent international commissions headed by world leaders such as Willy Brandt of Germany, Olof Palme of Sweden, Julius Nyerere of Tanzania, Gro Harlem Brundtland of Norway, and Ingvar Carlsson of Sweden prompted a fundamental rethinking of security. Out of these efforts evolved two closely linked concepts: *common security*—the view that in order for one state to be secure, its opponents must also feel secure; and *comprehensive security*—the notion that non-military factors such as social inequity, poverty, environmental degradation, and migratory pressures are at least as important as military ones in determining the potential for conflict. Questions have been raised as to whether many sources of conflict today are at all amenable to military solutions, a perspective currently being discussed under the heading *human security*.[83]

The years since the end of the Cold War have seen a reduction in military spending; in production, trade, and deployment of arms; and in the size of armed forces. Yet progress has been highly uneven across the world, substantial arsenals remain in place, there is no letup in the drive toward more sophisticated weaponry, and business in transferring both new and "surplus" weapons from one country to another is still brisk.

Fundamentally, little has changed as far as reliance on armed forces is concerned. The utility of military power has hardly been foresworn by the world's governments. The Clinton Administration asserts that today's instabilities must be combatted by military means. Its recent request for an additional $112 billion for the Pentagon during the next six years (2000–2005) reverses the trend of recent years and is sure to influence decisionmaking in other capitals around the world, steering us in the wrong direction.[84]

A key task in the twenty-first century will be to establish effective restraints based on three principles. These principles contrast sharply with the approaches underlying past and present policies: disarmament (as opposed to arms control); universal constraints on arms (as opposed to non-proliferation); and war prevention (as opposed to regulating warfare).

Although the world has pulled back from the nuclear brink, disarmament is needed as never before. There are still few internationally accepted norms to curb the production, possession, or trade of arms. Several decades of arms control efforts have yielded mostly weak numerical limits on the numbers of certain weapons that states may deploy, and no limits at all on many other kinds of arms. The list of weapons that have actually been outlawed since 1899, when the Hague International Peace Conference decided to ban expanding, or so-called dum dum, bullets, is extremely short compared to the list of unregulated weapons. Although the use of chemical weapons was banned in 1925 (a norm violated several times), nearly another 70 years passed before the 1993 Chemical Weapons Convention outlawed their production and possession. In 1995 the sale and use of so-called blinding-laser weapons was banned, and a treaty prohibiting anti-personnel landmines, signed in 1997, came into force in 1999.[85]

Now that there are no big-power confrontations and few armed conflicts between states, an unparalleled opportunity beckons for far-reaching disarmament in both the nuclear and the conventional realms. Denuclearization— the establishment of a timetable to phase out and eventually eliminate all nuclear arms—is one of the pressing tasks in coming years. The nuclear "haves" not only insist that they will retain their arsenals indefinitely, they continue to pursue modernization programs, and their existing arsenals remain on hairtrigger alert. But the stakes are rising: India and

The list of weapons that have actually been outlawed since 1899 is extremely short.

Pakistan have joined the "nuclear club," and it is overly optimistic to assume that others will not eventually be tempted to re-evaluate their policies and to acquire nuclear weapons as well. Even if no government is contemplating starting a nuclear war intentionally, other dangers lurk, among them accidental launchings of missiles and theft of nuclear weapons or related materials and technology by terrorists or non-nuclear states.[86]

In light of today's dominant types of conflicts, an equally urgent task is to adopt restraints on the conventional arms trade. Huge amounts of weapons of all calibers have been dispersed all over the planet. Among the most worrisome aspects of this buildup is the widespread proliferation of small arms—the weapon of choice in today's internal fighting.

One measure long demanded by human rights organizations and other groups is a binding code of conduct to ensure that, at the very least, weapons are not exported to governments that fail to hold free elections, that trample human rights or engage in armed aggression. A voluntary code of conduct was adopted by the European Union in June 1998, but it remains to be seen whether the region's governments will live by it or ignore it when the code proves inconvenient. Establishing effective, binding codes in Europe and elsewhere remains a crucial step toward peace. However, in the next century, we will need to aim for an even more ambitious goal: establishing a normative presumption against trading arms altogether, so that such transfers are no longer seen as routine commercial transactions but rather as highly unusual events.[87]

It is also time to rethink the utility of large standing military forces and to advance the norm that possession of an offensively armed military is unacceptable. Countries that face no obvious external adversaries may want to cut their militaries radically and to refocus remaining forces on purely defensive tasks; indeed, some may want to reconsider whether they need an army at all, joining the twentieth-century pioneers Costa Rica, Haiti, and Panama in abolishing their standing armed forces. Unilateral measures by individual countries could create some badly needed momentum, but far-reaching progress would likely depend on a more systematic, multilateral approach. An NGO initiative, "Global Action to Prevent War," is proposing a four-phase process over 20–40 years to achieve major reductions in armies and their armaments. Following extensive consultations among non-governmental experts, it will be formally launched at the Hague Appeal for Peace conference in May 1999.[88]

The second general principle concerns universality of norms. In order to be just and effective, constraints on armaments need to apply to all states equally. This contrasts with the nonproliferation policies that are currently in vogue in Western nations—the idea of allowing a select (and self-appointed) group of countries to hold on to certain kinds of weapons denied to all other states. Nuclear arsenals are the most prominent example. The Non-Proliferation Treaty prohibits the acquisition of nuclear arms by nations that do not now possess them—the vast majority of the world's countries. Yet the nuclear weapons states have shown little inclination to fulfill their part of the bargain and begin serious negotiations for nuclear abolition. The advanced nations are also working hard to establish a monopoly on sophisticated arms technologies (although this goal is often contradicted by their active non-nuclear export salesmanship). The upshot is a kind of global security apartheid system.[89]

This kind of lopsided approach to security is not only unacceptable from the perspective of universality, it is also unworkable in the long run. As long as one country or group of countries has access to a weapon, others will be tempted to acquire it as well. No matter what the true utility of the weapon in question may be, the very fact that one government prizes its possession signals to others that it must have direct military value, heighten a country's influence, or provide some other, less tangible, advantage. This may be a fool's game, but it is one that states have played for centuries. At best, pursuing such policies into the future is an enormous waste of resources; at worst, it could spawn new arms races and trigger regional or global instabilities.

The third principle, preventing war, also requires dramatic change. At the 1899 Hague conference, governments expressed their "desire to diminish the evils of war so far as military necessities permit," a desire that remained unfulfilled. Although war laws could be made more stringent, the past 100 years have demonstrated that there is an inherent limit to how effective they can be. Rather than trying in vain to make war a "chivalrous" affair, it is far more fruitful to focus on preventing violent conflict. Yet while government leaders give occasional lip service to conflict prevention, far too little is being done to make it happen. For instance, in 1997 the newly established U.N. Trust Fund for Preventive Action Against Conflicts received soaring rhetoric but scant funds.[90]

Much could be accomplished by building an early conflict warning network, establishing permanent dispute arbitration centers in every region of the world, giving more backing to preventive diplomacy, and establishing a corps of skilled and experienced individuals to serve as roving mediators on behalf of the international community. Conflict prevention is not an exact science, to be sure; instead, it resembles a trial-and-error process. On the one hand, there will be cases when early warning of impending violent conflict turns out to be a false alarm. On the other hand, though, the international community would do well to have some redundancy built into the conflict prevention apparatus, so that a variety of efforts aimed at warding off mass violence can be launched. Preventing the eruption of disputes into full-scale hostilities is by no means an easy task, but its difficulties pale beside those of ending fighting once extensive bloodshed has occurred.

Of course, conflict prevention through mediation will not always work, so additional tools are needed. In particular, peacekeeping missions will need to be refashioned so that they can embody the true meaning of the word peace-*keeping*, instead of serving as last-minute fire brigades. In the course of the last few years, we have come to associate peacekeeping with hapless efforts—too few people equipped too poorly and dispatched too late, unable to keep a peace that scarcely exists on the ground. What is needed is the creation of a well-trained, permanent force under U.N. auspices for preventive deployments. It would be dispatched in response to clear signs of imminent violent dispute, either along national borders or even within countries. Such an intervention should not be seen as an end in itself, but rather be designed to provide space for mediation efforts.[91]

In a fast-paced world that prefers lightning-quick action with decisive outcomes, there is aversion to the typically open-ended commitments that prevention and mediation require and the compromises and nuances without which conflict resolution is unlikely to succeed. Political leaders are tempted to assume that military strikes—such as those against Serbia intended to change its policy on Kosovo—offer a quick, clearcut alternative. But this is a questionable proposition. Even where this policy has been executed in the most straightforward manner—trying to force Iraq's Saddam Hussein to come clean on his weapons of mass destruction programs, for instance—the result is ambiguous at best. Bombing raids now preclude international monitoring of Iraqi sites suspected of harboring prohibited weapons programs. In Kosovo as well, bombing may punish Slobodan Milosevic (or, more likely, Serbia's civilian population), but it is unlikely to succeed in halting Serb "ethnic cleansing," let alone bring about an arrangement that will allow Serbs and Kosovars to live together peacefully. Without patient and early commitment, conflicts cannot be resolved.[92]

Far-reaching disarmament, universally applied constraints on armaments, and vigorous conflict prevention efforts will go a long way toward addressing the more traditional aspects of a peace policy. But to be successful, these steps will need to be linked with a broader human security agenda. Conflict prevention is not only about positioning peacekeepers between would-be attackers and their intended victims (though a few successful operations of that kind could have a salutary effect), but more fundamentally about recognizing and ameliorating the underlying pressures that lead to violent disputes in the first place.

At the core, the shift toward prevention calls for policies that are geared to strengthening the fabric of society and improving its governance. Central to such a policy are goals like fair distribution of wealth and balancing of the interests of different population groups, adequate job creation, poverty eradication, and the preservation or restoration of ecosystems. These are urgent requirements in a world in which the simultaneous presence of tremendous economic growth and widespread inequity is driving environmental destruction, breeding explosive social conditions, and fueling ethnic antagonisms.[93]

Governments will need to adopt policies better able to stem the degradation of watersheds and arable lands, to conserve and protect critical natural systems, and to pursue climate stabilization policies. Key to success also are measures to boost the efficiency with which energy, materials, and water are used. In developing countries where a large share of the population depends directly on the integrity and stability of ecosystems, the benefits would not only be environmental, but would also carry over into the social and political realms by helping to avoid the dislocations and distributive conflicts that now go hand in hand with wholesale environmental destruction. But industrial countries' policies are critical as well, since they consume the bulk of the world's resources and are thus, directly or indirectly, responsible for the preponderance of unsustainable mining, logging, metal smelting, fishing, and fossil fuel burning.[94]

It is equally important that governments become more serious about fulfilling pledges to eradicate poverty, promote full employment, and reduce massive social inequality. At the World Social Summit in Copenhagen in 1995, it was widely recognized that social conditions are closely linked to issues of peace. But the summit's rhetoric has so far proved stronger than actual policy commitments. Only with strong NGO involvement will it be possible to translate rhetorical pledges into reality.[95]

In an age in which capital-intensive technology and planetary-wide economies of scale combine to limit the potential for job creation even as the ranks of job-seekers keep swelling, a fundamental re-assessment of employment policies is overdue. This concerns questions such as the choice of appropriate technology, the need to tax energy and resource consumption rather than labor, and the design of fiscal and subsidy policies. Budgetary priorities need re-examining as well; as long as massive resources continue to be invested in the military, for example, social needs will always be given short shrift.[96]

National governments, though often embattled, can do much on their own to promote human security and reduce the potential for conflict. However, because human existence is increasingly shaped by both globalizing and localizing trends, there is a need both to promote greater international cooperation and to give civil society a far greater role in setting the agenda.

As the repercussions of world market integration from Indonesia to Russia to Brazil have become unmistakable, it is clear that the orthodox free-market approach that emphasizes the supremacy of freedom of trade and capital movements over all other goals ill serves the need for social, economic, and ultimately political stability. A key task now is to minimize the disruptive features of global economic integration and, where necessary, to adopt some deliberate limits to it. This does not mean moving from one extreme—a virtually unconditional embrace of global market forces—to another—protectionism—but rather underscores the need for a more selective approach, recognizing that market demands sometimes clash with the imperatives of sound social policy.

Conflict prevention calls for policies that are geared to strengthening the fabric of society and improving its governance.

In the orthodox view, the current litmus test of governmental policy is how swiftly it proceeds with deregulation and privatization and how much it facilitates trade and capital flows. The result may well be a boosted gross national product. But these goals have been pushed far too single-mindedly. From a human security perspective, what counts is whether the general well-being of the population is served without overexploiting nature, leaving certain communities behind, or undermining local culture, customs, and norms. Global economic integration does not always lead to adverse outcomes, but it is time to require something that might be described as social and environmental impact statements of globalization. Global economic integration will not turn into a race to the bottom if strong environmental and social standards can be developed; establishing high common-denominator norms on the global level will be one of the major challenges in coming years.[97]

Seen basically as protections against state oppression, human rights need to be understood also as tools to protect the economically and socially weak from the depredations of the strong. Human rights, broadly understood, are of growing importance in a globalizing world, as decisionmaking processes affect larger and larger numbers of individuals and communities in more and more profound ways. The world's political and corporate elites have been far more interested, and effective, in creating a global market structure than they have been in establishing three essential conditions that are critical to preventing globalization from becoming a continuous source of contention: first, making the most powerful market players more accountable; second, preparing the ground on which a global human community, not just a global market place, can flourish; and third, setting up sufficiently strong international institutions that can help advance global norms and safeguard the interests of the global human community.

The international institutions vested with the greatest degree of authority and power—the International Monetary Fund and the World Trade Organization among them—not only lack transparency and accountability in their decision-making, but sometimes devote themselves to the pursuit of economic growth even at the direct expense of social, environmental, and human rights considerations. Grassroots activists have been working hard to change the way these institutions operate, but more reform is still necessary.

Considerable expectations for achieving and safeguarding the global community are being pinned on the United Nations, whose various departments and agencies are involved in many activities crucial to improving the welfare of people. Yet, the U.N. receives scant resources and commands little political power. Half a century after its founding, the organization that was set up to prevent recurring war is increasingly in danger of being emasculated, particularly by U.S. reluctance to pay its dues to the organization. Because the entire U.N. system—headquarters, specialized agencies, and peacekeeping operations—is owed about $3.6 billion in outstanding dues from member states, it has languished in financial crisis for several years now. In the new

century, governments will need to provide full and generous
funding to the U.N. if they want it to be a more effective
voice for peace than it has been to date.[98]

To that end, reform is as essential as new money. The
Security Council, for instance, is increasingly anachronistic
in its composition and central workings—particularly the
veto power retained by the five permanent members. But
although discussions have been held for years and there is
no shortage of good reform proposals, there is no consensus
on the specifics. The permanent members are highly reluc-
tant to relinquish or water down any of their privileges, espe-
cially their veto power. If they succeed in blocking timely
change, they will further increase worldwide resentment of
outdated privileges. Since the Council relies on the willing
cooperation of the world's nations, a rejection of reform may
over time compromise its authority and effectiveness.[99]

Because security policy will increasingly need to move
beyond military issues in the next century and concern itself
with the social, economic, demographic, and environmental
pressures that are at the root of most conflicts, the United
Nations system as a whole will be critical to success. But like
the Security Council, it needs reforming. And as is the case
with Council reform, no consensus has emerged from
amongst an endless number of reform proposals—some
intended to strengthen the U.N., others to limit its role.[100]

One of the most important challenges is to make the
U.N. less an organization of government representatives and
more one of the "peoples of the United Nations," as the U.N.
Charter puts it. As mentioned earlier, NGOs are already playing a growing role at many international venues and conferences. But their rising influence will need to find clearer
institutional expression at the United Nations itself, perhaps
by moving toward a multi-chamber system and adding to the
General Assembly one or more assemblies that are more
broadly representative of each society. This could entail a par-
liamentary chamber (with representatives elected directly in
each nation, as the members of the European Parliament are),
and a forum of civil society that includes representatives of

labor, environmental groups, and others. Such a change
would not be an entirely revolutionary concept: the ILO has
long had a tripartite structure, bringing together representatives of government, business, and labor.[101]

Impatient with the failure of governments to promote
conflict prevention and peace building, NGOs—or civil society organizations as they are increasingly called—are playing
a more and more assertive role on the local, national, and
international levels. And in an age in which peace and security concerns are focused more on internal than on interstate
matters, it is only sensible that civil society should be an
active participant.

Recent years have seen the emergence of working coalitions that, on an issue-by-issue basis, bring together NGOs
with like-minded governments. The anti-personnel landmines campaign is the outstanding example of this phenomenon. With the support of countries like Canada, South
Africa, Belgium, and Norway, the campaign succeeded in
putting landmines on the global agenda, hammering out an
international treaty banning these devices, and bringing it
into force at a speed far faster than any other arms treaty in
history.

Although the landmines campaign was in many ways
unique, its stunning success naturally prompted hopes that
it could be replicated in other areas. Similar themes rever-
berate in the efforts to establish an International Criminal
Court, the gathering campaign to counter small arms proliferation, and the "Middle Powers Initiative" (an endeavor to
encourage nuclear-weapons states to commit to practical
steps toward the elimination of their atomic arsenals).
Whatever their eventual outcome, these efforts are helping
to revolutionize the process of international policymaking
by infusing it with human rights, humanitarian, and human
development concerns to a far greater extent than has been
the case to date.[102]

Canadian Foreign Minister Lloyd Axworthy has been a
particularly vocal proponent of this new "pulpit diplomacy,"
which regards NGO activists as a vanguard of change; opens

traditionally quiet (and often secretive and slow-moving) diplomacy to far greater scrutiny and mobilizes public opinion; and frequently takes the initiative from the big powers, putting them into the unaccustomed position of having to play catch-up. Soft power, as it is also called, is based on the notion that human security, not state security, should be the organizing principle of peace policy; it regards military force as having declining utility; and it emphasizes the power of ideas and the promulgation of new norms over the power of weapons.[103]

NGO input may well be crucial to establishing human security. A century ago, states were in their prime. But already, citizen activists like Bertha von Suttner were beginning to stir and "intrude" into what was then considered the preserve of statecraft. Although pacifists succeeded in convincing governments to convene the 1899 Hague conference, despite intense petitioning efforts, as outsiders they had little influence over its outcome. Since then, the situation has changed dramatically. Today, NGO representatives are frequent participants at intergovernmental gatherings. The 1999 Hague Appeal for Peace conference goes even farther: it is an attempt to set the agenda for twenty-first-century peacemaking at which government and U.N. representatives are welcome guests, but not the initiators.

Notwithstanding valiant efforts to the contrary, the twentieth century was the century of warfare. The twenty-first will need to be the century of demilitarization and conflict prevention. As South African Archbishop and Nobel Prize recipient Desmond Tutu has pointed out, slavery once seemed like an immutable reality and yet it was abolished. "Why not war? Indeed, we have no choice."[104]

Notes

1.   Armaments increase from Eric Hobsbawm, *The Age of Empire: 1875-1914* (New York: Vintage Books, 1989), and from Paul Kennedy, *The Rise and Fall of the Great Powers* (New York: Vintage Books, 1987); Nobel from Brigitte Hamann, *Bertha von Suttner: A Life for Peace* (Syracuse, NY: Syracuse University Press, 1996).

2.   Hamann, op. cit. note 1.

3.   Ibid.; czar quote from Charles Chatfield and Ruzanna Ilukhina, eds., *Peace/Mir: An Anthology of Historic Alternatives to War* (Syracuse, NY: Syracuse University, 1994).

4.   Hague conference from Hamann, op. cit. note 1; "1899–1928: The Hague Convention," <http://www.lib.byu.edu/~rdh/wwi/hague.html>, viewed 20 July 1998. Agreement was reached to ban the dropping of weapons from balloons—warplanes were yet to be developed—for a limited number of years, but this ban was allowed to lapse. International Committee of the Red Cross (ICRC), "Declaration (XIV) Prohibiting the Discharge of Projectiles and Explosives from Balloons, The Hague, 18 October 1907," <http://www.icrc.ch/unicc/ihl_eng.nsf/>, viewed 13 August 1998.

5.   Hobsbawm, op. cit. note 1.

6.   The effect of population growth and social change in rural and urban areas one century ago is discussed in William H. McNeill, *The Pursuit of Power: Technology, Armed Force, and Society since A.D. 1000* (Chicago: University of Chicago Press, 1982).

7.   The beginning of World War I presents a perfect example of how military imperatives overrode all other considerations. Military historians point out that once the order for war mobilization was issued in 1914, "there was no drawing back. Everything had to go like clockwork. Any effort to interfere would jam the works at once ... Hence, subordination of military action to political considerations ... became completely impossible." In the case of Germany "no one, not even the kaiser, could change the plan once war had been decided on. Similar rigidities also arose in France, Russia, and Austria ..." per McNeill, op. cit. note 6. The Kosovo conflict offers an illustration of the dangers lurking in today's rigidities. Western powers bet everything on the threat of air strikes against Serbia in order to deter "ethnic cleansing" against Kosovo's ethnic Albanian majority. This, however, led to the need to withdraw international observers and the media from Kosovo, giving Serb paramilitary forces an opportunity to spread terror with impunity. In effect, NATO narrowed its own options to either stepping up its already massive air attacks or calling them off entirely. Either response may fail to bring about stated objectives, namely protecting the civilian popula-

tion of Kosovo. See, for example, R.W. Apple, "Bombs Fall, Goal Unmet?" *New York Times*, 28 March 1999.

8. Hague Appeal for Peace, "International Campaign Launched to Abolish War in the New Century," press release (New York: 1 March 1999).

9. Moltke cited in Hamann, op. cit. note 1.

10. Grey quoted in James Trager, *The People's Chronology: A Year-by-Year Record of Human Events from Prehistory to the Present* (New York: Henry Holt and Co., 1994).

11. Preambles from Louise Doswald-Beck and Sylvain Vité, "International Humanitarian Law and Human Rights Law," web site of the International Committee of the Red Cross, <http://www.icrc.ch/unicc/icrnews.nsf/>, viewed 13 August 1998; "Declaration Renouncing the Use, in Time of War, of Certain Explosive Projectiles: St. Petersburg, 29 November/11 December 1868," <http://www. lib.byu.edu/~rdh/wwi/1914m/gene68.html>, viewed 20 July 1998; 1899 declaration from Chatfield and Ilukhina, op. cit. note 3.

12. Table 1 from William Eckhardt, "War-Related Deaths Since 3000 BC," *Bulletin of Peace Proposals*, December 1991, and from Ruth Leger Sivard, *World Military and Social Expenditures 1996* (Washington, DC: World Priorities, 1996).

13. Trager, op. cit. note 10; Eric Hobsbawm, *The Age of Extremes: A History of the World, 1914–1991* (New York: Vintage Books, 1994); Richard M. Garfield and Alfred I. Neugut, "The Human Consequences of War," in Barry S. Levy and Victor W. Sidel, eds., *War and Public Health* (New York: Oxford University Press, 1997). Table 2 compiled from Ruth Leger Sivard, *World Military and Social Expenditures 1991* (Washington, DC: World Priorities, 1991).

14. John Keegan, *The Second World War* (New York: Penguin Books, 1989); Martin van Crefeld, *The Transformation of War* (New York: Free Press, 1991). 65 million and 1 percent figure calculated from Kennedy, op. cit. note 1.

15. Number of airplanes from Patrick D. Stobart, *Centenary of the Hall & Heroult Processes, 1886–1986* (London: International Primary Aluminum Institute, 1986); Hobsbawm, op. cit. note 13; Trager, op. cit. note 10; van Crefeld, op. cit. note 14.

16. Van Crefeld, op. cit. note 14; living standards from Angus Maddison, *Monitoring the World Economy 1820–1992* (Paris: Organisation for Economic Co-operation and Development, 1995).

17. Maddison, op. cit. note 16; Hobsbawm, op. cit. note 13.

18. Stobart, op. cit. note 15.

19. Soldiers from John Elting, U.S. Military Academy, "Costs, Casualties, and Other Data," Grolier Online World War II Commemoration, <http://www.grolier.com/wwii/wwii_16.html>, viewed 22 July 1998; 45 million figure is a Worldwatch estimate based on data in Office of the Undersecretary of Defense (Comptroller), *National Defense Budget Estimates for FY 1996* (Springfield, VA: National Technical Information Service, March 1995), in Alan L. Gropman, *Mobilizing U.S. Industry in World War II*, McNair Paper 50 (Washington, DC: Institute for National Strategic Studies, August 1996), and in van Crefeld, op. cit. note 14.

20. Number of tanks and aircraft calculated from Gropman, op. cit. note 19, from "A World of Tanks," <http://www.geocities.com/Pentagon/Quarters/1975/>, viewed 22 July 1998, and from Kennedy, op. cit. note 1. Aircraft figure includes Italy. Table 3 is based on Gropman, op. cit. note 19.

21. Soviet production from McNeill, op. cit. note 6; Hobsbawm, op. cit. note 13; Keegan, op. cit. note 14.

22. 52 million figure calculated from Sivard, op. cit. note 12; Hobsbawm, op. cit. note 13; Keegan, op. cit. note 14.

23. Stephen Schwartz, ed., A*tomic Audit: The Costs and Consequences of U.S. Nuclear Weapons since 1940* (Washington, DC: Brookings Institution Press, 1998).

24. Robert S. Norris and William M. Arkin, "Known Nuclear Tests Worldwide, 1945-1998," Nuclear Notebook, *Bulletin of the Atomic Scientists,* November/December 1998; Figure 1 is based on Robert S. Norris and William M. Arkin, "Global Nuclear Stockpiles, 1945–1997," Nuclear Notebook, *Bulletin of the Atomic Scientists,* November/December 1997; explosive force from Sivard, op. cit. note 12.

25. Number of missiles from "Missile Index," <http://www.index.ne.jp/missile_e/whatis.html>, viewed 31 July 1998; escalating cost from Sivard, op. cit. note 13.

26. 1988 and 1993 figures from Bonn International Center for Conversion (BICC), *Conversion Survey 1996: Global Disarmament, Demilitarization and Demobilization* (New York: Oxford University Press, 1996). Between 1946 and 1997, the United States spent a total of $1.4 trillion (in 1996 dollars) on military R&D programs per Office of the Undersecretary of Defense (Comptroller), op. cit. note 19. Global figure of $3.5 trillion is a Worldwatch Institute calculation, assuming that the United States accounted for 40 percent of the global total.

27. Paul Kennedy reports World War I expenditures of $82.4 billion (in 1913 dollars), or roughly $1.4 trillion (in 1998 dollars), Kennedy, op. cit. note 1. The International Institute for Strategic Studies (IISS), by contrast, reports a figure of $2.35 trillion in 1995 dollars (equaling $2.5 trillion in 1998 dollars).

See IISS, "The 1998 Chart of Armed Conflict," issued in conjunction with *The Military Balance 1998/99* (London: Oxford University Press, October 1998). Early 1930s from Sivard, op. cit. note 13; late 1930s calculated from Kennedy, op. cit. note 1. U.S. expenditures during 1940-45 amounted to about $2.5 trillion in 1998 dollars, calculated on basis of Executive Office of the President of the United States, *Historical Tables: Budget of the United States Government, Fiscal Year 1990* (Washington, DC: U.S. Government Printing Office (GPO), 1989). Extrapolation from U.S. to global spending based on assumption that United States accounted for about 40 percent of global World War II expenditures. Cold War military expenditures from U.S. Arms Control and Disarmament Agency (ACDA), *World Military Expenditures and Arms Transfers 1996* (Washington, DC: GPO, July 1997). Conversion into 1998 dollars by Worldwatch Institute, using U.S. Consumer Price Index (CPI) deflator series as reported by Robert Sahr, "Inflation Conversion Factors," <http://www.orst.edu/Dept/pol_sci/fac/ sahr/sahr.htm>, viewed 10 February 1999. Clearly the CPI is per se not an appropriate deflator, because it measures inflation for a basket of consumer goods, rather than military items. However, there appear to be no proper deflator series that reach back to the early parts of the 20th century; in the absence of such a series, the CPI at least provides a rough measure.

28. $1.5 trillion figure is a Worldwatch estimate, based on various editions of ACDA, *World Military Expenditures and Arms Transfers* (Washington, DC: GPO, various editions), and on Sivard, op. cit. note 12; 1984–95 transfers from ACDA, op. cit. note 27.

29. Figure 2 is based on data in Michael Renner, "Wars Increase Once Again," in Lester R. Brown, Michael Renner, and Brian Halweil, *Vital Signs 1999* (New York: W.W. Norton & Company, forthcoming, 1999); Table 4 from Sivard, op. cit. note 12; Korea and Vietnam population losses from Garfield and Neugut, op. cit. note 13.

30. Margareta Sollenberg, ed., *States in Armed Conflict 1997* (Uppsala, Sweden: Uppsala University, Department of Peace and Conflict Research, 1998).

31. Ian Fisher with Norimitsu Onishi, "Congo's Struggle May Unleash Broad Strife to Redraw Africa," *New York Times*, 12 January 1999.

32. Grotius quote from Chatfield and Ilukhina, op. cit. note 3. The provisions and full texts of many relevant agreements, treaties, and conventions can be found on various sites on the World Wide Web; most of them are maintained by university departments. See "Multilaterals Project Chronological Index," <http://tufts.edu/fletcher/multi/chrono.html>, viewed 29 July 1998 (Fletcher School of Law and Diplomacy; contains a page with links to other relevant treaty collections). Many international treaties are deposited with the United Nations Secretary-General, and the U.N. maintains a Treaty Collection that can be accessed online: <http://www.un.org/Depts/ Treaty/overview.htm>, viewed 29 July 1998.

33. Van Crefeld, op. cit. note 14; Dieter Fleck, ed., *The Handbook of Humanitarian Law in Armed Conflicts* (New York: Oxford University Press, 1995); Doswald-Beck and Vité, op. cit. note 11. Table 5 is based on U.N., op. cit. note 32, on Ian Browline, ed., *Basic Documents on Human Rights* (Oxford, U.K.: Clarendon Press, 1992), on Fleck, op. cit. this note, and on "Multilaterals Project Chronological Index," op. cit. note 32.

34. "Convention on the Prohibition of Military or Any Other Hostile Use of Environmental Modification Techniques," <http://www.tufts.edu/fletcher/multi/texts/BH700.txt>, viewed 17 August 1998; Doswald-Beck and Vité, op. cit. note 11.

35. Military success in preventing stronger war laws from Hans Blix, *Development of International Law Relating to Disarmament and Arms Control since the First International Peace Conference of 1899*, Preliminary Report Prepared for the 1999 Centennial of the First International Peace Conference, 1998; Croatia events from Raymond Bonner, "War Crimes Panel Finds Croat Troops 'Cleansed' Serbs," *New York Times*, 21 March 1999.

36. Teheran Conference quoted in Doswald-Beck and Vité, op. cit. note 11.

37. U.N., *Human Rights: A Compilation of International Instruments* (New York: 1978); U.N. Treaty Collection web site, <http://www.un.org/Depts/Treaty/final/ts2/newfiles/frontboo/toc4.htm>, viewed 19 August 1998; Browline, op. cit. note 33; Doswald-Beck and Vité, op. cit. note 11.

38. U.N. Department of Public Information (UNDPI), *Charter of the United Nations and Statute of the International Court of Justice* (New York: April 1994).

39. Growth of intergovernmental organizations from Allen Sens and Peter Stoett, *Global Politics* (New York: ITP Nelson, 1998).

40. UNDPI, op. cit. note 38; veto record from Michael Renner, "U.N. Peacekeeping Contracts Further," in Lester R. Brown, Michael Renner, and Christopher Flavin, *Vital Signs 1998* (New York: W.W. Norton & Company, 1998).

41. Michael Renner, "Peacekeeping Expenses Reach New High," in Lester R. Brown, Nicholas Lenssen, and Hal Kane, *Vital Signs 1995* (New York: W.W. Norton & Company, 1995).

42. Michael Renner, *Critical Juncture: The Future of Peacekeeping*, Worldwatch Paper 114 (Washington, DC: Worldwatch Institute, May 1993).

43. Michael Renner, "U.N. Peacekeeping Expenditures Drop More," in Brown et al., op. cit. note 29; U.N. General Assembly, "Administrative and Budgetary Aspects of the Financing of the United Nations Peacekeeping Operations," A/52/837, New York, 20 March 1998; Judith Miller, "Security Council Relegated to Sidelines," *New York Times*, 14 March 1999.

44. FAO from Chatfield and Ilukhina, op. cit. note 3; UNESCO Charter in <http://www.unesco.org>, viewed 28 June 1998; ILO Preamble, <http://www.ilo.org/public/english/overview/iloconst.htm>, viewed 15 August 1998; Nobel Peace prizes awarded to U.N. agencies and officials from "Major Achievements of the United Nations," <http://www.un.org/Overview/achieve.html>, viewed 10 August 1998, and from <http://www.nobel.se>, viewed 2 April 1998.

45. Web site of the International Court of Justice, <http://www.icj-cij.org/igeninf/ibbook/>, viewed 1 August 1998; Sens and Stoett, op. cit. note 39.

46. Monique Chemillier-Gendreau, "The International Court of Justice between Politics and Law," *Le Monde Diplomatique*, November 1996, with English version available at <http://www.globalpolicy.org/wldcourt/icj.htm>.

47. Benjamin B. Ferencz, *From Nuremberg to Rome: Towards an International Criminal Court,* Policy Paper 8 (Bonn: Development and Peace Foundation, May 1998).

48. Lawyers Committee for Human Rights, "Basic Principles For an Independent and Effective International Criminal Court (ICC)" <http://www.lchr.org/icc/paplist.htm>, viewed 20 July 1998; Iain Guest, "Beyond Rome—What are the Prospects for the International Criminal Court?" *On the Record,* 27 July 1998; "A Court Is Born," *On the Record,* 17 July 1998; number of signatories and parties from "Rome Statute of the International Criminal Court: Ratification Status," <http://www.un.org/law/ icc/statute/status.htm>, updated 17 March 1999; U.S. position from Alessandra Stanley, "U.S. Presses Allies to Rein in Proposed War Crimes Court," *New York Times,* 15 July 1998, and from Alessandra Stanley, "U.S. Dissents, but Accord is Reached on War-Crime Court," *New York Times,* 18 July 1998. Table 6 based on Human Rights Watch, "Human Rights Watch Text Analysis International Criminal Court Treaty July 17, 1998," <http://www.hrw.org/hrw/press98/july/icc-anly.htm>, viewed 12 August 1998, on "The Draft Statute at a Glance," *On the Record,* 27 July 1998, and on "A Court is Born," op. cit. this note.

49. Military expenditures from BICC, *Conversion Survey 1998: Global Disarmament, Defense Industry Consolidation and Conversion* (New York: Oxford University Press, 1998); armed forces from ACDA, op. cit. note 27; late 1980s figure for soldiers on foreign soil from Ruth Leger Sivard, *World Military and Social Expenditures 1987–88* (Washington, DC: World Priorities, 1987); mid-1990s from Michael Renner, "Armed Forces Continue Demobilizations," in Lester R. Brown, Michael Renner, and Christopher Flavin, *Vital Signs 1997* (New York: W.W. Norton & Company, 1997); arms exports from ACDA, *World Military Expenditures and Arms Transfers 1997* <http://www.acda.gov/wmeat97/wmeat97.htm>, viewed 28 March 1999.

50. Warheads from Norris and Arkin, op. cit. note 24; destructive power from Sivard, op. cit. note 12; other developments from Institute for Defense and Disarmament Studies (IDDS), *The Arms Control Reporter* (Cambridge, MA: various editions).

51. "A Brief History of Chemical Disarmament," <http://www.opcw. nl/basic>, viewed 7 August 1998.

52. Chatfield and Ilukhina, op. cit. note 3; Ervin Laszlo and Jong Youl Yoo, exec. eds., *World Encyclopedia of Peace*, Volume 3 (New York: Pergamon Press, 1986).

53. The oldest and most comprehensive international network of peace groups, the International Peace Bureau (IPB), functions to this day and currently has 160 member organizations worldwide; together, the office and its leaders have received a total of 14 Nobel Peace Prizes. "IPB History: Over a Century of Peacemaking," <http://www3.itu.ch/ipb/history/ history.htm>, viewed 2 April 1998; Laszlo and Yoo, op. cit. note 52.

54. World Court ruling from "Legality of the Threat or Use of Nuclear Weapons," <http://www.igc.apc.org/disarm/wcadop.html>, viewed 31 July 1998.

55. 1909 from Commission on Global Governance, *Our Global Neighborhood* (New York: Oxford University Press, 1995); 1956 from Union of International Organizations, *Yearbook of International Organizations 1996–1997* (Munich: K.G. Saur Verlag, 1997); 1996 from John Boli and George M. Thomas, "World Culture in the World Polity: A Century of International Non-Governmental Organization," *American Sociological Review,* April 1997. Unfortunately, these sources do not distinguish between bona fide grassroots NGOs and those that are affiliated with, or financed by, businesses. Number of NGOs with accreditation at the U.N. from P.J. Simmons, "Learning to Live with NGOs," *Foreign Policy,* fall 1998.

56. Simmons, op. cit. note 55. For an even more skeptical view, see David Rieff, "The False Dawn of Civil Society," *The Nation,* 22 February 1999. Churchill from Rhoda Thomas Tripp, *The International Thesaurus of Quotations* (New York: Harper & Row, 1970).

57. Van Crefeld, op. cit. note 14.

58. Map is based on Arbeitsgemeinschaft Kriegsursachenforschung (AKUF), Institute for Political Science, University of Hamburg, AKUF web site, <http://www.sozialwiss.uni-hamburg.de/Ipw/Akuf/ home.html>, viewed 4 January 1999.

59. Michael T. Klare, "The Era of Multiplying Schisms: World Security in the Twenty-First Century," in Michael T. Klare and Yogesh Chandrani, eds., *World Security: Challenges for a New Century* (New York: St. Martin's Press, 1998); Michael Renner, *Fighting for Survival: Environmental Decline, Social*

Conflict, and the New Age of Insecurity (New York: W.W. Norton & Company, 1996).

60. McNeill, op. cit. note 6; migration from Maddison, op. cit. note 16; Hobsbawm, op. cit. note 1.

61. Channeling of antagonisms toward external enemies from McNeill, op. cit. note 6.

62. Global disparities from U.N. Development Programme (UNDP), *Human Development Report 1994* (New York: Oxford University Press, 1994).

63. ILO, *World Employment Report 1998–99* (Geneva: 1998); ILO, "Economically Active Population 1950–2010," STAT Working Papers, No. 96-5 (Geneva: 1996).

64. Youth unemployment from ILO, op. cit. note 63.

65. Rwanda from Human Rights Watch, *Slaughter Among Neighbors: The Political Origins of Communal Violence* (New Haven, CT: Yale University Press, 1995); Kosovo from Chris Hedges, "Victims Not Quite Innocent," *New York Times*, 28 March 1999.

66. ILO, op. cit. note 63.

67. Ibid.; Russia from Stephen F. Cohen, "Why Call it Reform?" *The Nation*, 7/14 September 1998; ILO, "Asian Labor Market Woes Deepening," press release (Geneva: 2 December 1998).

68. Renner, op. cit. note 59; Thomas F. Homer-Dixon, *Environment, Scarcity, and Violence* (Princeton: Princeton University Press, 1999).

69. For a more detailed discussion, see Renner, op. cit. note 59; for case studies see Thomas Homer-Dixon and Valerie Percival, Project on Environment, Population, and Security, *Environmental Scarcity and Violent Conflict: Briefing Book* (Toronto and Washington, DC: University of Toronto and American Association for the Advancement of Science, 1996); Kurt R. Spillmann and Günther Bächler, eds., *Environmental Crisis: Regional Conflicts and Ways of Cooperation,* Occasional Paper No. 14 (Bern, Switzerland: Environment and Conflicts Project (ENCOP), September 1995); Günther Bächler et al., *Umweltzerstörung: Krieg oder Kooperation?* (Münster, Germany: Agenda Verlag, 1993).

70. Christopher Flavin, "Weather-Related Losses Hit New High," in Brown, et al., op. cit. note 29.

71. Klare, op. cit. note 59; India from Volker Böge, "Das Sardar-Sarovar-Projekt an der Narmada in Indien—Gegenstand ökologischer Konflikts," Occasional Paper No. 8 (Bern, Switzerland: ENCOP, June 1993).

72. Aid to El Salvador from Mireya Navarro, "Clinton to Begin Visit to Central America," *New York Times*, 7 March 1999.

73. Disintegration of armies, in sub-Saharan African context, discussed in Alex de Waal, "Contemporary Warfare in Africa," *IDS Bulletin*, vol. 27, no. 3 (1996); lack of Marshall Plan-type assistance from Liisa L. North, "The Challenge of Demobilization: The Construction of Peace and Regional Security," in Francisco José Aguilar Urbina, ed., *Demobilization, Demilitarization, and Democratization in Central America* (San José, Costa Rica: Arias Foundation for Peace and Human Progress, Centre for Peace and Reconciliation, 1994).

74. Commodity price indices from World Bank, *World Development Indicators 1998 on CD-ROM* (Washington, DC: 1998).

75. For a discussion of imperial overstretch through history, see Kennedy, op. cit. note 1.

76. James N. Rosenau, "The Dynamism of a Turbulent World," in Klare and Chandrani, op. cit. note 59.

77. Herman E. Daly, "Globalization and National Defense," Letter to the Editor, *World Watch*, November/December 1998.

78. Van Crefeld, op. cit. note 14.

79. William Greider, "The Global Crisis Deepens: Now What?" and John Gray, "Not for the First Time, World Sours on Free Markets," both in *The Nation*, 19 October 1998.

80. Dimensions of the downside to global economic integration are explored by David C. Korten, *When Corporations Rule the World* (West Hartford, CT: Kumarian Press, 1995), by Jerry Mander and Edward Goldsmith, eds., *The Case Against the Global Economy and for a Turn Toward the Local* (San Francisco: Sierra Club Books, 1996), by William Greider, *One World, Ready or Not: The Manic Logic of Global Capitalism* (New York: Touchstone, 1998), and by Benjamin R. Barber, *Jihad vs. McWorld* (New York: Ballantine Books, 1995).

81. Michael T. Klare discusses the privatization of security and violence in "The Global Trade in Light Weapons and the International System in the Post-Cold War Era," in Jeffrey Boutwell, Michael T. Klare, and Laura W. Reed, eds., *Lethal Commerce: The Global Trade in Small Arms and Light Weapons* (Cambridge, MA: Committee on International Security Studies, American Academy of Arts and Sciences, 1995); growth of private security forces and militarization of police in selected countries from Michael Renner, *Small Arms, Big Impact: The Next Challenge of Disarmament*, Worldwatch Paper 137 (Washington, DC: Worldwatch Institute, October 1997). In China, several hundred thousand soldiers have been transferred into a paramilitary police force, the People's Armed Police, which is charged, among other things, with containing the rising number of demonstrations and protests around the country per Erik Eckholm, "A Secretive Army Grows to Maintain Order in China," *New York Times*, 28 March 1999.

82. Van Crefeld, op. cit. note 14; Trager, op. cit. note 10.

83. For a concise discussion of the commissions' work, see Robert C. Johansen, "Building World Security: The Need for Strengthened International Institutions," in Klare and Chandrani, op. cit. note 59. The term "human security" has been popularized in particular by the *Human Development Report*, published annually by the UNDP.

84. Michael T. Klare, "The Clinton Doctrine," *The Nation*, 19 April 1999. Center for Defense Information, "The Fiscal Year 2000 Pentagon Budget Request,"<http://www.cdi.org/issues/usmi/highlightsFY00.html>, viewed 21 March 1999.

85. "1899–1928: The Hague Convention," op. cit. note 4; ICRC, op. cit. note 4, viewed 13 August 1998; Chemical Weapons Convention, the convention banning anti-personnel landmines, and the blinding-laser prohibition from IDDS, *Arms Control Reporter 1997* (Cambridge, MA: 1997).

86. Brian Hall, "Overkill Is Not Dead," *New York Times Magazine*, 15 March 1998; Jonathan Schell, "The Gift of Time," *The Nation*, 2/9 February 1998; Arjun Makhijani, "Achieving Enduring Nuclear Disarmament," *Science for Democratic Action* (Takoma Park, MD: Institute for Energy and Environmental Research, October 1998); Jaswant Singh, "Against Nuclear Apartheid," *Foreign Affairs*, September/October 1998.

87. The European Union (EU) code is reprinted in Joseph Di Chiaro III, *Reasonable Measures: Addressing the Excessive Accumulation and Unlawful Use of Small Arms,* Brief 11 (Bonn: Bonn International Center for Conversion, August 1998). For a critical analysis, see Saferworld, "The EU Code of Conduct on the Arms Trade: Final Analysis," <http://www.gn.apc.org/SWORLD/ARMSTRADE/ code.html>, viewed 5 October 1998.

88. Costa Rica, Haiti, and Panama from Joaquin Tacsan, "Reports on Projects and Activities of the Center for Peace and Reconciliation," in Arias Foundation for Peace and Human Progress, *Arias Foundation for Peace and Human Progress Performance Report 1988–1996* (San José, Costa Rica: 1996); Jonathan Dean, Randall Forsberg, and Saul Mendlovitz, "Global Action to Prevent War: A Program for Government and Grassroots Efforts to Stop War, Genocide, and Other Forms of Deadly Conflict," Union of Concerned Scientists, IDDS, and World Order Models Project, 15 September 1998.

89. On the principle of universality, see Johansen, op. cit. note 83.

90. Hague conference quoted in Blix, op. cit. note 35. In 1997, the U.N.

Trust Fund received just $4.5 million, from the Netherlands and Norway; Trevòr Findlay, "Armed Conflict Prevention, Management and Resolution," in Stockholm International Peace Research Institute (SIPRI), *SIPRI Yearbook 1998: Armaments, Disarmament and International Security* (New York: Oxford University Press, 1998).

91. For a detailed discussion of conflict prevention needs and opportunities, see Carnegie Commission on Preventing Deadly Conflict, *Preventing Deadly Conflict: Final Report* (New York: Carnegie Corporation, 1997). For a more detailed discussion of peacekeeping reform, see Renner, op. cit. note 42.

92. On Iraq, see Jonathan S. Landay, "After Raids on Iraq, UN in Turmoil," *Christian Science Monitor*, 24 December 1998. On Kosovo, see Jan Øberg, "Bombings Incompatible with Humanitarian Concerns," Press Info No. 60, 24 March 1999, Transnational Foundation for Peace and Future Research, Lund, Sweden.

93. These policy requirements are discussed at greater length in Renner, op. cit. note 59.

94. Disproportionate Western resource consumption from Aaron Sachs, "Upholding Human Rights and Environmental Justice," in Lester R. Brown et al., *State of the World 1996* (New York: W.W. Norton & Company, 1996).

95. U.N., "Report of the World Summit for Social Development (Copenhagen, 6–12 March 1995)," New York, 19 April 1995; Social Watch, *Social Watch: The Starting Point* (Montevideo: 1996); Social Watch <http://www.socwatch.org.uy/1998/english/index.html>, viewed 25 March 1999.

96. On tax and subsidy issues, see David Malin Roodman, *The Natural Wealth of Nations: Harnessing the Market for the Environment* (New York: W.W. Norton & Company, 1998).

97. For example, Klaus Töpfer, Executive Director of the U.N. Environment Programme, announced in early 1999 that "UNEP will make a priority in the coming years to collect empirical data as to the environment consequences of international economic policies," in "High Level Symposium of Trade and Environment: Statement of the Executive Director of UNEP," <http://www.wto.org/wto/hlms/topfer.htm>, viewed 16 March 1999.

98. Michael Renner, "U.N. Peacekeeping Expenditures Drop More," and "U.N. Finances Decline Further," in Brown et al., op. cit. note 29.

99. Phyllis Bennis, *Calling the Shots: How Washington Dominates Today's UN* (New York: Olive Branch Press, 1996). For documents and further discussion of reform efforts, see the Global Policy Forum web site, <http://www.globalpolicy.org/reform/analysis.htm>, viewed 21 March 1999.

100. For a large number of U.N. reform-related documents, see Global Policy Forum, op. cit. note 99. Also see the U.N.'s own web site <http://www.un.org/reform>.

101. NGO consultative status discussions are covered by Global Policy Forum, op. cit. note 100; for forward-looking proposals, see Johansen, op. cit. note 83; Commission on Global Governance, op. cit. note 55.

102. Robert D. Green, *Fast Track to Zero Nuclear Weapons: The Middle Powers Initiative* (Cambridge, MA: The Middle Powers Initiative, 1998).

103. Fen Osler Hampson and Dean F. Oliver, "Pulpit Diplomacy: A Critical Assessment of the Axworthy Doctrine," *International Journal*, summer 1998; Steven Pearlstein, "Canada's New Age of Diplomacy," *Washington Post*, 20 February 1999.

104. Tutu quoted in United Nations Foundation, *UN Wire*, 12 March 1999, <http://www.unfoundation.org/unwire/unwire.cfm>.

Worldwatch Papers

No. of Copies

Worldwatch Papers by Michael Renner

_____146. **Ending Violent Conflict** by Michael Renner

_____137. **Small Arms, Big Impact: The Next Challenge of Disarmament** by Michael Renner

_____122. **Budgeting for Disarmament: The Costs of War and Peace** by Michael Renner

_____145. **Safeguarding The Health of Oceans** by Anne Platt McGinn

_____144. **Mind Over Matter: Recasting the Role of Materials in Our Lives**
by Gary Gardner and Payal Sampat

_____143. **Beyond Malthus: Sixteen Dimensions of the Population Problem**
by Lester R. Brown, Gary Gardner, and Brian Halweil

_____142. **Rocking the Boat: Conserving Fisheries and Protecting Jobs** by Anne Platt McGinn

_____141. **Losing Strands in the Web of Life: Vertebrate Declines and the Conservation of
Biological Diversity** by John Tuxill

_____140. **Taking a Stand: Cultivating a New Relationship with the World's Forests**
by Janet N. Abramovitz

_____139. **Investing in the Future: Harnessing Private Capital Flows for Environmentally
Sustainable Development** by Hilary F. French

_____138. **Rising Sun, Gathering Winds: Policies to Stabilize the Climate and Strengthen
Economies** by Christopher Flavin and Seth Dunn

_____136. **The Agricultural Link: How Environmental Deterioration Could Disrupt Economic
Progress** by Lester R. Brown

_____135. **Recycling Organic Waste: From Urban Pollutant to Farm Resource** by Gary Gardner

_____134. **Getting the Signals Right: Tax Reform to Protect the Environment and the Economy**
by David Malin Roodman

_____133. **Paying the Piper: Subsidies, Politics, and the Environment** by David Malin Roodman

_____132. **Dividing the Waters: Food Security, Ecosystem Health, and the New Politics of
Scarcity** by Sandra Postel

_____131. **Shrinking Fields: Cropland Loss in a World of Eight Billion** by Gary Gardner

_____130. **Climate of Hope: New Strategies for Stabilizing the World's Atmosphere**
by Christopher Flavin and Odil Tunali

_____129. **Infecting Ourselves: How Environmental and Social Disruptions Trigger
Disease** by Anne E. Platt

_____128. **Imperiled Waters, Impoverished Future: The Decline of Freshwater Ecosystems**
by Janet N. Abramovitz

_____127. **Eco-Justice: Linking Human Rights and the Environment** by Aaron Sachs

_____126. **Partnership for the Planet: An Environmental Agenda for the United Nations**
by Hilary F. French

_____125. **The Hour of Departure: Forces That Create Refugees and Migrants** by Hal Kane

_____124. **A Building Revolution: How Ecology and Health Concerns Are Transforming
Construction** by David Malin Roodman and Nicholas Lenssen

_____123. **High Priorities: Conserving Mountain Ecosystems and Cultures**
by Derek Denniston

_____121. **The Next Efficiency Revolution: Creating a Sustainable Materials Economy**
by John E. Young and Aaron Sachs

_____120. **Net Loss: Fish, Jobs, and the Marine Environment** by Peter Weber

_____119. **Powering the Future: Blueprint for a Sustainable Electricity Industry**
by Christopher Flavin and Nicholas Lenssen

_____118. **Back on Track: The Global Rail Revival** by Marcia D. Lowe

_____117. **Saving the Forests: What Will It Take?** by Alan Thein Durning

_____116. **Abandoned Seas: Reversing the Decline of the Oceans** by Peter Weber

_____**Total copies (transfer number to order form on next page)**

PUBLICATION ORDER FORM

NOTE: Many Worldwatch publications can be downloaded as PDF files from our website at **www.worldwatch.org**. Orders for printed publications can also be placed on the web.

_____ *State of the World:* **$13.95**
The annual book used by journalists, activists, scholars, and policymakers worldwide to get a clear picture of the environmental problems we face.

_____ **State of the World Library: $30.00 (international subscribers $45)**
Receive *State of the World* and all five Worldwatch Papers as they are released during the calendar year.

_____ *Vital Signs:* **$13.00**
The book of trends that are shaping our future in easy-to-read graph and table format, with a brief commentary on each trend.

_____ **WORLD WATCH magazine subscription: $20.00 (international airmail $35.00)**
Stay abreast of global environmental trends and issues with our award-winning, eminently readable bimonthly magazine.

_____ **Worldwatch Database Disk Subscription: $89.00**
Contains global agricultural, energy, economic, environmental, social, and military indicators from all current Worldwatch publications. Includes a mid-year update, and *Vital Signs* and *State of the World* as they are published. Disk contains Microsoft Excel spreadsheets 5.0/95 (*.xls) for Windows.
Check one: _____ **PC** _____ **Macintosh**

_____ **Worldwatch Papers—See list on previous page**
Single copy: $5.00
2–5: $4.00 ea. • 6–20: $3.00 ea. • 21 or more: $2.00 ea.

$4.00* Shipping and Handling *($8.00 outside North America)*
minimum charge for S&H; call (800) 555-2028 for bulk order S&H

_____ **TOTAL** (U.S. dollars only)

Make check payable to: Worldwatch Institute, 1776 Massachusetts Ave., NW, Washington, DC 20036-1904 USA

Enclosed is my check or purchase order for U.S. $_____

☐ AMEX ☐ VISA ☐ MasterCard _____
Card Number   Expiration Date

_____
signature

_____
name   **daytime phone #**

_____
address

_____
city   **state**   **zip/country**

phone: (800) 555-2028   **fax: (202) 296-7365**   **e-mail: wwpub@worldwatch.org**
website: www.worldwatch.org

Wish to make a tax-deductible contribution? Contact Worldwatch to find out how your donation can help advance our work.

Worldwatch Papers

No. of Copies

Worldwatch Papers by Michael Renner

_____146. **Ending Violent Conflict** by Michael Renner
_____137. **Small Arms, Big Impact: The Next Challenge of Disarmament** by Michael Renner
_____122. **Budgeting for Disarmament: The Costs of War and Peace** by Michael Renner

_____145. **Safeguarding The Health of Oceans** by Anne Platt McGinn
_____144. **Mind Over Matter: Recasting the Role of Materials in Our Lives**
by Gary Gardner and Payal Sampat
_____143. **Beyond Malthus: Sixteen Dimensions of the Population Problem**
by Lester R. Brown, Gary Gardner, and Brian Halweil
_____142. **Rocking the Boat: Conserving Fisheries and Protecting Jobs** by Anne Platt McGinn
_____141. **Losing Strands in the Web of Life: Vertebrate Declines and the Conservation of
Biological Diversity** by John Tuxill
_____140. **Taking a Stand: Cultivating a New Relationship with the World's Forests**
by Janet N. Abramovitz
_____139. **Investing in the Future: Harnessing Private Capital Flows for Environmentally
Sustainable Development** by Hilary F. French
_____138. **Rising Sun, Gathering Winds: Policies to Stabilize the Climate and Strengthen
Economies** by Christopher Flavin and Seth Dunn
_____136. **The Agricultural Link: How Environmental Deterioration Could Disrupt Economic
Progress** by Lester R. Brown
_____135. **Recycling Organic Waste: From Urban Pollutant to Farm Resource** by Gary Gardner
_____134. **Getting the Signals Right: Tax Reform to Protect the Environment and the Economy**
by David Malin Roodman
_____133. **Paying the Piper: Subsidies, Politics, and the Environment** by David Malin Roodman
_____132. **Dividing the Waters: Food Security, Ecosystem Health, and the New Politics of
Scarcity** by Sandra Postel
_____131. **Shrinking Fields: Cropland Loss in a World of Eight Billion** by Gary Gardner
_____130. **Climate of Hope: New Strategies for Stabilizing the World's Atmosphere**
by Christopher Flavin and Odil Tunali
_____129. **Infecting Ourselves: How Environmental and Social Disruptions Trigger
Disease** by Anne E. Platt
_____128. **Imperiled Waters, Impoverished Future: The Decline of Freshwater Ecosystems**
by Janet N. Abramovitz
_____127. **Eco-Justice: Linking Human Rights and the Environment** by Aaron Sachs
_____126. **Partnership for the Planet: An Environmental Agenda for the United Nations**
by Hilary F. French
_____125. **The Hour of Departure: Forces That Create Refugees and Migrants** by Hal Kane
_____124. **A Building Revolution: How Ecology and Health Concerns Are Transforming
Construction** by David Malin Roodman and Nicholas Lenssen
_____123. **High Priorities: Conserving Mountain Ecosystems and Cultures**
by Derek Denniston
_____121. **The Next Efficiency Revolution: Creating a Sustainable Materials Economy**
by John E. Young and Aaron Sachs
_____120. **Net Loss: Fish, Jobs, and the Marine Environment** by Peter Weber
_____119. **Powering the Future: Blueprint for a Sustainable Electricity Industry**
by Christopher Flavin and Nicholas Lenssen
_____118. **Back on Track: The Global Rail Revival** by Marcia D. Lowe
_____117. **Saving the Forests: What Will It Take?** by Alan Thein Durning
_____116. **Abandoned Seas: Reversing the Decline of the Oceans** by Peter Weber

_____**Total copies (transfer number to order form on next page)**

PUBLICATION ORDER FORM

NOTE: Many Worldwatch publications can be downloaded as PDF files from our website at **www.worldwatch.org**. Orders for printed publications can also be placed on the web.

_____ *State of the World:* **$13.95**
The annual book used by journalists, activists, scholars, and policymakers worldwide to get a clear picture of the environmental problems we face.

_____ **State of the World Library: $30.00 (international subscribers $45)**
Receive *State of the World* and all five Worldwatch Papers as they are released during the calendar year.

_____ *Vital Signs:* **$13.00**
The book of trends that are shaping our future in easy-to-read graph and table format, with a brief commentary on each trend.

_____ **WORLD WATCH magazine subscription: $20.00 (international airmail $35.00)**
Stay abreast of global environmental trends and issues with our award-winning, eminently readable bimonthly magazine.

_____ **Worldwatch Database Disk Subscription: $89.00**
Contains global agricultural, energy, economic, environmental, social, and military indicators from all current Worldwatch publications. Includes a mid-year update, and *Vital Signs* and *State of the World* as they are published. Disk contains Microsoft Excel spreadsheets 5.0/95 (*.xls) for Windows.
Check one: _____ **PC** _____ **Macintosh**

_____ **Worldwatch Papers—See list on previous page**
Single copy: $5.00
2–5: $4.00 ea. • 6–20: $3.00 ea. • 21 or more: $2.00 ea.

$4.00* Shipping and Handling *($8.00 outside North America)*
minimum charge for S&H; call (800) 555-2028 for bulk order S&H

_____ **TOTAL** (U.S. dollars only)

Make check payable to: Worldwatch Institute, 1776 Massachusetts Ave., NW, Washington, DC 20036-1904 USA

Enclosed is my check or purchase order for U.S. $_____

☐ AMEX ☐ VISA ☐ MasterCard _____
Card Number   Expiration Date

signature
_____

name   **daytime phone #**
_____

address
_____

city   **state**   **zip/country**

phone: (800) 555-2028   fax: (202) 296-7365   e-mail: wwpub@worldwatch.org
website: www.worldwatch.org

Wish to make a tax-deductible contribution? Contact Worldwatch to find out how your donation can help advance our work.